D0790974

# Inspiring
# Devotions
# for Church Groups

# Inspiring Devotions for Church Groups

## Amy Bolding

**BAKER BOOK HOUSE**
Grand Rapids, Michigan 49506

Copyright 1968, 1976, 1985 by Baker Book House Company

Library of Congress Catalog Card Number: 68-29785

ISBN: 0-8010-0889-1

Second printing, November 1986

These devotions were selected from *Day by Day with Amy Bolding*.

Printed in the United States of America

## New Year, New Start

*"But as it is written, Eye hath not seen nor ear heard, neither have entered into the heart of man, the things which God hath prepared for them that love him."* — I Corinthians 2:9

We have come to a new year; a year to invest in happiness, a new year to invest in service and love. Let us forgive all that is in the past, and look forward to a bright handful of tomorrows. Isn't it fun to have a surprise! It makes a day brighter. We like so much to have surprise parties for those we love. God has a wonderful year of surprises awaiting those who love him.

We will enjoy these things which God has prepared for us more if we lay aside all littleness that may have kept us from doing our best in the past and determine to give our best in the year ahead. Shall we resolve to do so?

> To be of greater service, Lord,
> A closer student of Thy Word;
> To help to bear a brother's load
> And cheer him on the heavenly road;
> To tell the lost of Jesus' love,
> And how to reach the home above;
> To trust in God whate'er befall,
> Be ready at the Master's call
> For any task that He may give;
> And thus through all the year to live
> For Him who gave Himself for me
> And taught me that my life should be
> A life unselfish, not self-willed,
> But with the Holy Spirit filled.

*Prayer*: Dear God, help us to accept with gratitude the measure of our days. Help us with grace to accept each day as a gift and use it to prepare for the eternal. We ask in the name of the giver of all days. Amen.

## The Path Ahead

*"Thou wilt show me the path of life: in thy presence is fulness of joy; at thy right hand there are pleasures forevermore."*
— Psalm 16:11

We have taken only a few steps on the road of our new year. How exciting! God's tomorrow has become God's today! The things which last week we planned to do next year are now ready to be started, for "next year" has become today. There is so much hopefulness in this day, so much promise, and so much excitement. It is time to begin what we had looked forward to doing. We are inevitably and steadily marching forward on this pathway of life. Let us walk carefully, for our footsteps cannot be retraced. Let us accept with joy the path before us.

Plan that today will be better than the days that have passed. Plan that the footstep you leave behind will guide someone who will follow.

> One small life in God's great plan,
> How futile it seems as the ages roll,
> Do what it may, or strive how it can,
> To alter the seep of the infinite whole!
> A single stitch in an endless web,
> A drop in the ocean's flow and ebb!
> But the pattern is rent where the stitch is lost,
> Or marred where the tangled threads have crossed;
> And each life that fails of its true intent
> Mars the perfect plan that the Maker meant.
>
> — Susan Coolidge

*Prayer*: As we start the pathway of a new year, dear Father, help us to submit our lives to thy will. Realizing our own helplessness, may we put our trust completely in thee. Help us to seek thy purpose for us and triumph in giving ourselves to the fulfilment of that purpose. Amen.

## Conforming Clay

*"We will keep his commandments, and do those things that are pleasing in his sight."* — I John 3:22

> Have Thine own way, Lord!
> Have Thine own way!
> Thou art the Potter;
> I am the clay.
> Mold me and make me
> After Thy will,
> While I am waiting
> Yielded and still.

God made the world after a divine plan, and for a divine purpose. In fact, he has a plan and purpose for each life. We cannot know God's plan and purpose for our life in advance, but we can trust that it is perfect and correct. In this confidence it is ours to keep his commandments and be pleasing to him.

We might think of ourselves as a vessel being fashioned and designed for his purpose. When we grow rebellious the design becomes blurred and ugly. We must learn to live with our past mistakes, but also ever to strive to make each day better as we submit to the Master's touch.

> Where deeds of mine can help
> To make this world a
> Better place for men to live in,
> Where word of mine can cheer
> A despondent heart or brace
> A weak will,
> Where prayer of mine can serve the
> Extension of Christ's kingdom
> There let me do and speak and pray!

*Prayer*: Almighty Father, we stand in need of protection from the enemies standing round about us. Help us ever to determine to keep thy commandments and in keeping them to live a better life of service and love. Amen.

## Tugboats for the Lord

*"Therefore if any man be in Christ, he is a new creature: old things are passed away; behold, all things are become new."*
— II Corinthians 5:17

> Today another challenge comes,
> In accents loud and clear:
> How am I going to spend my life
> Throughout the coming year?
> Shall I for self and pleasure live,
> And listless pass the days?
> Or shall I live for Christ, the Lord,
> And render Him my praise?
> Lord, I would spend this year for Thee,
> So, help me as I try;
> My Saviour's smile — the glorious prize
> Awaits me bye and bye.
> — Marie L. Olson

We may classify people into three groups. First we think of the people who have to be pushed or shoved along. They never have enough energy to get busy and do worthwhile things on their own. They remind us of a rowboat without anyone to row or push it along — useless unless helped by others.

Then there is a group of people who remind us of a sailboat. It moves along very well when the wind is blowing in a favorable direction. These people like to be with the crowd and work as the crowd works. They must have wind for their sails if they are to accomplish anything.

The third group reminds us of a tugboat. Through storm or calm they go right on doing what they know is right. They make the world a better place in which to live and work. For them each new day is a day of service for God and man.

We choose the kind of people we will be.

*Prayer*: Father, as the winds of life buffet me about, help me, that I may be led of thee to be firm and true to thy kingdom work. Inspire me to love those about me in such a way that they too will want to be a new creature in Christ. Grant thy special blessing upon those who are slow or who are going only with popular currents. Help them to trust in thee. For in the name of the one who makes us new we pray. Amen.

## Christ is Our Traveling Companion

*"Then they willingly received him into the ship: and immediately the ship was at the land whither they went."* — John 6:21

I was sitting in the car after church — just watching people as they left. Then I saw a young couple come out of the door. They were holding hands, and from the way they looked at each other I knew they must be in love. The boy was a stranger to me, but I had known the girl, a college senior, since she was very small.

As I watched them with warmth in my heart, I suddenly remembered. That same young girl had called the week before to tell me that as soon as graduation was over she was going to a foreign land to be a missionary helper for two years.

My heart felt heavy. She would go for the two years when most girls are having a good time, choosing husbands, and getting married. I knew too that her parents were not happy about her decision. Then the thought of today's Scripture verse came to my mind. With Christ as her traveling companion the time would seem short. She would be a blessing to many people and there would still be young men in America when she returned. In fact, the one who was holding her hand might not mind waiting for her return.

The sea of life grows smooth when we have Christ as our traveling companion.

Others may do a greater work,
But you have your part to do;
And no one in all God's heritage
Can do it so well as you.

*Prayer*: Dear Lord, bless those who are serving thee, whether here at home, or far away. In Jesus' name we pray. Amen.

## Step by Step

*"Order my steps in thy word: and let not any iniquity have dominion over me."* — Psalm 119:133

When I was a child my parents tried to teach me what was right and what was wrong. I did not always do just the right thing, and at times I was punished for disobedience. Then suddenly I was grown up, and when a question of right or wrong arose I had to make the decision myself. Even in adulthood I found that one is punished if one chooses the wrong path. More and more, as I developed as a Christian, I found it best to ask God to order my steps — I found it best to depend upon him for guidance. When my steps were ordered by the Lord I found my life happier and more complete. You, too, will find this to be true.

He does not lead me year by year
Not even day by day,
But step by step my path unfolds,
My Lord directs the way.
Tomorrow's plans I do not know
I only know this minute!
But He will say, "This is the way,
By faith now walk ye in it."
And I am glad that it is so;
Today's enough to bear.
And when tomorrow comes, His grace
Shall far exceed its care.

*Prayer*: Dear Father, exceeding and abundant are thy gifts to us each day. Help us to be grateful for thy blessings; for thy guiding hand along life's way. We rejoice in the glorious hope we have for tomorrow; for the promises of thy sufficiency and care. For we pray in the name of Christ. Amen.

## God's Love Does Not Slow Down

*"Herein is love, not that we loved God, but that he loved us, and sent his Son to be the propitiation for our sins."*

— I John 4:10

Josephine Skaggs, a missionary in Nigeria, was told by a friend to "slow down." She replied: "It isn't what we do that hurts us; it's what we can't do. It is the knowledge that over the next hill there are multitudes who would respond, as others have, if we could but go to them. But there aren't enough hours in the day, nor is there enough strength in the human frame to meet their appalling needs."

This missionary loves so much that she is literally wearing out her body in her zeal to tell others about Christ's love. God has such a wonderful love for a lost world that he made a way of redemption for us. He literally poured out his love for us. God is able to save from the uttermost and to the uttermost.

Oh what love! How can we "slow down" — or sit still?

> If I have moved a single grain of sand
> This day to help my fellow man,
> If I have brought one stray into the fold,
> Or sent a ray of hope to one lonely soul
> Like a sunbeam in a prison cell;
> Or on the desert sands a water well
> To quench his anguish on the way of life,
> Or ease his heartbreak in the battle strife —
> This day is not lost.

— Patricia Soito

*Prayer*: Father, we thank thee for the wonderful people of the earth who are willing to spend their lives in service far from home. Bless them today. We ask in Christ's name. Amen.

## "The Glory of Friendship"

*"Two are better than one; because they have a good reward for their labor. For if they fall, the one will lift up his fellow: but woe to him that is alone when he falleth; for he hath not another to help him up."* — Ecclesiastes 4:9, 10

Ralph Waldo Emerson wrote: "The glory of friendship is not the outstretched hand, nor the kindly smile, nor the joy of companionship; it is the spiritual inspiration that comes to one when he discovers that someone else believes in him and is willing to trust him with his friendship."

We should try *to be* a helpful friend. To be a good friend one must have clean thoughts and noble purposes. If we deal justly with those around us, tell the truth, and show fine conduct, people want us for their friends.

We should strive *to have* good friends. They offer encouragement when we are discouraged; they offer to share our joys when we are glad. They keep life from being barren and lonely.

Some folks hunger for a friend,
　　For friends make life worthwhile;
And other hearts are hungry
　　For just a pleasant smile.
Kind words and deeds have wondrous power
　　To save a soul from sin;
To drive the threatening clouds away
　　And let the sunshine in.

*Prayer*: For our friends we are grateful. Send us out to be more friendly to those in need of help. May people never reach out in vain asking our friendship. We ask in the name of the greatest friend man has known. Amen.

## A Jewel of a Day

*"If thou turn away thy foot from the sabbath, from doing thy pleasure on my holy day; and call the sabbath . . . the holy of the Lord . . . and shalt honor him, not doing thine own ways, nor finding thine own pleasure, nor speaking thine own words: then thou shalt delight thyself in the Lord. . . ."* — Isaiah 58:13, 14

We should plan for Sunday to be different from all the other days in the week. If we truly love God and delight in serving him we will observe Sunday as he asks us to. Sunday should be a day for worship, a day for resting, a day for fellowship with friends in the Lord's house. Sunday should be a day of helpfulness to others.

Sunday should be the day we are quiet and listen to God speak. We will be thankful for his blessings if we have a quiet time to meditate on them.

In many ways we disregard God's will for this one day in seven. In early days of America, without the aid of modern refrigerators, the housewife prepared the food on the day before. She, too, rested on Sunday.

God gave us Sunday as a precious jewel hanging on the chain of the week. We should guard the way we use it.

Safely through another week
God has brought us on our way;
Let us now a blessing seek,
Waiting in His courts today;
Day of all the week the best,
Emblem of eternal rest:

While we pray for pardoning grace,
Through the dear Redeemer's name,
Show thy reconciled face;
Take away our sin and shame:
From our worldly cares set free,
May we rest this day in Thee.

— John Newton

*Prayer*: Father, how grateful we are that we can say, "Thy word is a lamp unto my feet, and a light unto my path." If we have been heedless in thy house, forgive us and make us true worshipers of thy son. We ask in Jesus' name. Amen.

## Encouragement: A Light in the Storm

*"I press toward the mark for the prize of the high calling of God in Christ Jesus."* — Philippians 3:14

Many years ago, in the early years of West Texas, people sometimes lived in dugouts. These were rooms dug down in the ground and covered over, with only a door leading outside. One day the teacher of a small one-room schoolhouse noticed the beginning of a snow storm. She dismissed school and told the children to hurry home as fast as they could. Three little children, who lived in a dugout two miles from the school, started for home. When it seemed to them they would never find their home because the snow was so thick, the little one began to cry from exhaustion and cold.

The two older ones were holding her hands and almost carrying her along. They, too, felt lost and helpless but wanted to be brave for her sake.

"Look! I see a light," one of them cried. Sure enough, they could see a faint light. "We will try to reach that light."

So they kept going with the faint glow of the light to guide them. Soon they reached home, guided by the light hanging high on their windmill. Their anxious mother had climbed to the top and hung a lighted lantern there.

Many people are near their goal in life but no one lights a lantern for them, and they falter on the way. Sometimes just a kind word of encouragement will help a fellow traveler.

*Prayer*: Help us, O God, to consecrate our lives to the giving of light to those who are in darkness. Let thy presence go with us today. We pray in the name of our Lord and Saviour. Amen.

## Still Providing "Manna"

*"Behold that which I have seen: it is good and comely for one to eat and to drink, and to enjoy the good of all his labor that he taketh under the sun all the days of his life, which God giveth him: for it is his portion."* — Ecclesiastes 5:18

We must admit we are inadequate without God. With God life is a big adventure. With him as our partner we need not be afraid. The person trusting in God is eager to see what is around the corner. He does not look forward with fear but with expectation of God's blessings.

It is wonderful when as children of God we can see all the beauties of life God has planned and prepared for us and be blind to a few discomforts along the way, knowing that God has a portion for us and it is good. The children of Israel were fed manna every day when they needed it. They found water when it was needed. All was provided by God who watched over them and cared for them. Do we not worship the same God? Is he not just as good and powerful today? He will provide for us.

In heavenly love abiding,
No change my heart shall fear,
And safe in such confiding,
For nothing changes here.
The storm may roar without me,
My heart may low be laid;
But God is round about me,
And can I be dismayed?
— Anna M. Waring

*Prayer*: O God, make us aware that each day is a precious gift from thee. Help us to reflect our love for thee in our relationship with our fellow men. May each day of our life have meaning for us and be spent in helping others. For it is in the name of Christ we pray. Amen.

## On Which Side of the Rope Are You Swimming?

*"For the which cause I also suffer these things: nevertheless I am not ashamed: for I know whom I have believed, and am persuaded that he is able to keep that which I have committed unto him against that day."* — II Timothy 1:12

In a youth camp I sometimes visit there is a swimming pool. The pool is divided into two parts by a rope. One part is shallow and the other part is deep. The lifeguard decides the part in which a child will be allowed to swim by whether or not the child knows how to dive. If a child can get on the diving board and dive into the deep water, he is considered ready for the deep part of the pool.

Will we go through life paddling around in shallow water — or will we launch out into the deep and try for big things? Some of us are afraid to try big things, fearful that we may fail. Others jump out into life and try over and over, trusting God to help them. If we take God with us we will find the deep water easier to conquer. We should never leave home in the morning without asking God to guide our steps that day. We should never come face to face with a major decision without asking God to help us make the right choice.

> It's glorious just to walk with God,
>   In fellowship so sweet;
> To revel in his presence as
>   Our souls the Saviour meet.
>
> His blessed Word is practical,
>   But it must be applied
> In ordinary daily tasks
>   Or else Christ is denied.
>
> Our lives are to embody him,
>   And live him forth each day,
> That all may see the difference in
>   The world's and Jesus' way.
>
> It is our wondrous privilege
>   God's temple here to be:
> The Spirit's living, earthly house
>   Where men, our Lord, may see.
>                               — J. T. Bolding

*Prayer*: Merciful Heavenly Father, give us wings that will lift us above the common things of earth into realms of heavenly places. Help us have courage to attempt big things. We ask in Jesus' name. Amen.

## Faith for Times of Friction

*"And we know that all things work together for good to them that love God, to them who are called according to his purpose."*
— Romans 8:28

Confucius said: "The gem cannot be polished without friction, nor man perfected without trials."

There are times when we think we have our life all planned, all cut out according to a certain pattern. Then tragedy or change comes and we find it necessary to go in another direction. At such a time we must remember the Scripture and know that Romans 8:28 is still in effect. It is still true: "All things work together for good to them that love God." God directs us — sometimes gently, sometimes roughly — but always he is pushing us toward his purpose for us.

> God grant that I may find my task,
>   And have the grace to do it well;
> And leave behind a stepping-stone,
>   To earth's triumphant citadel.
>
> Keep firm my faith and strong my grasp
>   On true perspective and the goal;
> That I may toil and weary not,
>   And be the captain of my soul.
>
> Let not the lure of fame or greed,
>   Make one dark blot upon my line;
> That each day's work be clean and good,
>   In keeping with Thy will and mine.
>
> God, grant that I may find my task,
>   And have the grace to do it well;
> And leave behind a stepping-stone,
>   Complete, unmarred, celestial.

— Alex Hoe

*Prayer*: Make us diligent toilers in thy vineyard. For in Christ's name we pray. Amen.

## First Aid for Divided Hearts

*"Their heart is divided; now shall they be found faulty."*

— Hosea 10:2

When someone is having serious physical trouble we rush him to the doctor or give first aid ourselves, if possible.

What can we do when someone has a divided heart? If we say we trust Christ, yet are trying to rely on ourselves for salvation, we have a divided heart. If we are trying to serve God and mammon, we have a divided heart.

We can render first aid to our hearts by depending on Christ solely for our redemption, by serving him with our whole heart.

The dark stream of evil is flowing apace;
Awake, and be doing, ye children of grace,
Let's seek with compassion the souls that are lost,
Well knowing the price their redemption has cost.
While singing with rapture the Saviour's great love,
And waiting for Him to translate us above —
"It may be tomorrow, or even tonight" —
Let our loins be well girded, and lamps burning bright.

*Prayer*: Help us O God, to give thee our whole heart. To serve thee in such a way that others will see our example and follow. Let us shake off the sloth of worldly ease and self-indulgence. We pray for the sake of Jesus Christ. Amen.

## Taking God for Granted

*"Watch therefore: for ye know not what hour your Lord doth come."* — Matthew 24:42

On a corner in West Texas there is a small house where children wait for the school bus. Billy is always the one who peeps out into the wind to see if the bus is coming. When he sees it far down the road he signals the others to gather up their books and be ready. If some child has not arrived yet, he pleads with the bus driver to wait just a moment for the late one. The children all laugh about Billy being so anxious about them. One day Billy was ill and could not go to school. The children in the little shelter felt lonely and cold. They missed Billy's ordering them about and being so concerned about them. The bus came and sounded the horn before they realized it was even near.

16

We take God's loving care for us so much for granted that we often forget to say thanks. Then one day when we are not watching, a dark shadow comes over our life and we realize how much God's love and protection means to us.

> The Lord has promised good to me,
> His Word my hope secure;
> He will my shield and portion be,
> As long as life endures.

*Prayer:* We thank thee, our Father, for the glorious gifts thou dost so bountifully bestow upon us. In Christ's name we pray. Amen.

## "Immortal Nightingales"

*"But these are written, that ye might believe that Jesus is the Christ, the Son of God; and believing ye might have life through his name."* — John 20:31

Books are written for many purposes. When I was a child I thought the First Reader was about the most important book in my life. As a teen-ager I often walked a mile to the public library in order to read and be with the books. John wrote his Gospel for a special purpose — to help people believe in Jesus Christ. That which you read may bless or curse you the rest of your life. Be very careful how you spend your reading time.

Richard Le Gallienne, an English author, said of books: "They are the immortal nightingales that sing forever."

Provide good reading for those who are your responsibility.

When you provide a Bible for someone you may be the means of changing the whole way of life for that person.

When you provide a book of inspiration about some great character you may encourage a genius.

"Books are the ever-burning lamps of accumulated wisdom," says G. W. Curtis.

### The Bible Contains:

The mind of God, the state of man, the way of life, the doom of sinners, the happiness of believers.

> Read it to be wise.
> Believe it to be safe.
> Practice it to be holy.

It gives the light to direct you, food to support you, and comfort to cheer you.

*Prayer*: Hide thy word in our hearts, O Lord, and fill us with thy love. In Christ's name. Amen.

## Defense Against Darts

*"Wherefore take unto you the whole armor of God, that ye may be able to withstand in the evil day, and having done all, to stand."* — Ephesians 6:13

One of my friends gave a party. I felt hurt because I did not receive an invitation. A few days after the party she asked me, "Why didn't you come?"

"I was not invited," I replied tartly.

A few days later the invitation came. The letter had been mis-sent to another address and I received it too late. The hurt I had felt in my heart had made a scar which did not heal quickly.

Someone hurts your feelings — so you want to give up and hide. That is not the way. Put on the whole armor of God and let the darts be bent as they push against it. There are goals in life to be reached. They cannot be reached if we do not have an armor against the bad and unhappy things we encounter along the way.

Most people at some time or other feel lonely, apprehensive, or uneasy. Put on your armor against these feelings.

Happiness is a sweet spring flowing from your devotion to God. The firmer is your devotion to God the stronger is your armor.

The grandstand is always full of people who criticize and tell the players how to play; but the ball game is won by the ones on the field, those putting forth the effort to win. Remember the ones who throw the darts are usually not in the game. Let their darts bounce off your armor, and stride forth with a firm deter-mination to win.

*Prayer*: Father, set our hearts aglow with the warmth of thy love. Infuse us with joy and peace. We pray in the name of Christ our Lord. Amen.

## Whose World Is It?

*"Therefore let no man glory in men. For all things are yours; whether Paul, or Apollos, or Cephas, or the world, or life, or death, or things present, or things to come; all are yours; and ye are Christ's; and Christ is God's."* — I Corinthians 3:21-23

18

"For all things are yours." What wonderful words! Yet to make all things ours we must live for the good of others. In the beginning of the world "God saw that it was good." We still live in a world that has much good in it. It is up to us to go out and make it ours. We must believe that there is still good to be found and accomplished in the world. Believing this we must make the good things ours — ours to enjoy, to give to others, to share with the sad, to enlighten the ignorant, to teach the unlearned, to lift up all those we meet.

To really make the world ours we must give ourselves completely to the Christ who paid the ransom for our sins.

> Drop a pebble in the water,
>   And its ripples reach out far;
> And the sunbeams dancing on them
>   May reflect them to a star.
>
> Give a smile to someone passing,
>   Thereby make his morning glad;
> It may greet you in the evening
>   When your own heart may be sad.
>
> Do a deed of simple kindness;
>   Though its end you may not see,
> It may reach, like widening ripples,
>   Down a long eternity.
>
> — Joseph Morris

*Prayer*: Make our lives today hospitable, and appreciative. Through Christ our Lord we pray. Amen.

## Taming Our Tempers

*"For he that will love life, and see good days, let him refrain his tongue from evil, and his lips that they speak no guile: Let him eschew evil, and do good; let him seek peace, and ensue it."*
— I Peter 3:10, 11

> When I have lost my temper
>   I have lost my reason, too,
> I am never proud of anything
>   Which angrily I do!
> In looking back across my life
>   And all I've lost or made,
> I can't recall a single time
>   When fury ever paid.

19

I have learned by sad experience
That when my temper flies,
I never do a worthy deed, or wise.

We should start each day with joy in our hearts and we should try to retain this spirit throughout the day. If we let someone make us angry and cause us to say ugly words we take away not only our own joy but the joy of others as well.

Perhaps when we grow angry with someone we have not stopped to consider that person's problems. He may be laboring under a heavy load and in need of a lift — not an angry word.

The Indians had a saying: "Never judge another until you have walked a week in his moccasins."

Sometimes we grow angry and say unkind words. We intend to ask forgiveness in a few moments, or at the end of the day. And then we forget or neglect doing so. Why not ask forgiveness at once. Why take the chance of leaving someone hurt and disappointed from our quick temper? Why hurt him at all?

Some people want to master a trade. Others want to develop a skill — or master an art. But we should all want to master our tempers.

*Prayer*: Bless us now, O God. Fill our hearts with prayer and meditation. We ask in Jesus' name. Amen.

## Carbon Copies

"*. . . And have put on the new man, which is renewed in knowledge after the image of him that created him.*"

— Colossians 3:10

People seem to want to be like the crowd. If some terrible crime is reported in the paper, in a few days there will be reports of similar crimes committed by people who were weak and acted on the power of suggestion. Christians must strive to be carbon copies of Christ, not of the world.

When we attempt to be carbon copies of some person we admire, or maybe even someone we fear, we too should ask the question, "Will I be willing to pay the price?" Jesus asked the disciples if they were able to suffer as he would suffer.

For many years all the young Baptist ministers tried to copy the late Dr. George Truett. But they could not in their preaching reach the heights that he reached. There was a reason unknown to most of them. They had not gone to the depths in suffering as he had gone. He had accidentally shot a friend on a hunting trip. From that day forward his life was more fully dedicated to service.

It is hard for parents to make their children see that some popular youth is not worthy of imitation. A parent knows that a wild youth will in all probability come to a sad end, but it is hard to make children realize that. They see the future only as the present looks. We must ever hold up the ideals and image of the one who created us.

Whom shall we take as an example — for ourselves, for our children?

*Prayer*: Father, let thy love be our companion on this pilgrimage of life. Strengthen our hearts with faith. We ask in the name of Christ. Amen.

## Those Little Things that Seem So Big

*"I can do all things through Christ which strengtheneth me."*
— Philippians 4:13

There are times when we need strength from above, not for some giant problem but just for the everyday, petty annoyances of life.

We have a friend who has his office in his home. He spent a tidy sum of money having a beautiful sign made and painted, and placed in his front yard. All went well until a family with five small children moved across the street. All through the day the children would run across the street and climb the man's sign. They got the letters all dirty and caused the sign to wobble from their weight. Our friend repeatedly had to take of his valuable time to go out and persuade the children to leave. He was a Christian and did not want to act unkindly. So as often as he went out he asked God to give him grace to act kindly but firmly. Only love of God and strength from above kept him from having an open feud with the children and their parents.

There are times when we must ask for strength to meet petty annoyances. If allowed to control our thoughts they can make us unhappy. Sometimes we have to ask God to make us deaf to the sound of a neighbor's barking dog when we need our sleep. Perhaps at times like these we should quote our Scripture for today.

*Prayer*: Lift us today, out of petty, trifling things; make us more like Christ our Saviour. For in His name we pray. Amen.

## Keeping Our Eyes Off the Giants

*"And there we saw the giants, the sons of Anak, which come of the giants; and we were in our own sight as grasshoppers, and so we were in their sight."* — Numbers 13:33

We should see our difficulties as opportunities for exercising faith in God. When we are like the Israelites, seeing only the giants, we are defeated. We must see the power of the God we serve.

It is a great tragedy to stand before a difficulty unprepared. Then we think only of dodging trouble, forgetting that dodging may bring even greater trouble.

One beautiful spring morning when my sister was driving to work a bee flew into her car. She became frightened and tried so hard to dodge the bee that she wrecked her car. If she had just driven along very quietly, the bee might have found a place to alight, and she would have avoided a large repair bill.

Do you fix your eyes upon God when troubles come? Be positive. Know that He is able to conquer the giants — and then trust Him to do so. Have faith in God.

> Simply trusting ev'ry day,
> Trusting through a stormy way;
> Even when my faith is small,
> Trusting Jesus, that is all.
>
> Brightly doth His Spirit shine,
> Into this poor heart of mine:
> While He leads I cannot fall;
> Trusting Jesus that is all.
>
> Singing if my way is clear;
> Praying if the path be drear;
> If in danger, for Him call;
> Trusting Jesus, that is all.
>
> Trusting Him while life shall last,
> Trusting Him till earth be past;
> Till within the jasper wall:
> Trusting Jesus, that is all.
>
> Trusting as the moments fly,
> Trusting as the days go by;
> Trusting Him what e'er befall,
> Trusting Jesus, that is all.
>
> — E. Page

*Prayer*: God of grace, may we find comfort in trusting thee today. We pray in the name of Jesus. Amen.

## Don't Forget Who's Master

*"And call no man your father upon the earth: for one is your Father, which is in heaven. Neither be ye called masters: for one is your Master, even Christ."* — Matthew 23:9, 10

Who is the master of your life?

The great preacher, Billy Sunday, used to say: "Wrong thinking makes everything wrong. Right thinking makes everything right." When we forget who is Master of our lives we are thinking wrongly.

Many people plan someday to give their heart to Christ but they think there are still many years ahead in which to make the Christ the Master of their lives. We have only today. There is no promise of tomorrow; so we must pick a master worth serving today. "Choose you this day whom you will serve."

It is truly wonderful to have Christ as the head of our lives. When problems arise and we seem to stand alone we need only to remember that Christ is our Master. Then we will not feel alone. He is a master worth serving. He can meet our every need.

*Prayer*: Fill us with a desire to serve men far and near. Bless our efforts as we try to serve. We pray in the name of Christ. Amen.

## Strong in the Wind

*"When thou shalt besiege a city a long time, in making war against it to take it, thou shalt not destroy the trees thereof by forcing an ax against them: for thou mayest eat of them, and thou shalt not cut them down (for the tree of the field is man's life) to employ them in the siege."* — Deuteronomy 20:19

How we all admire a tree grown straight and tall! But we seldom stop to think of the many years it takes a tree to grow and develop.

One spring we had an unusually large number of bad windstorms. A young apricot tree just outside our back door was especially windblown. Some days it seemed as if we would have to cut the lush green top out in order to save our prized tree from blowing down altogether. My husband took soft rags and ropes and anchored it to stakes. With the ropes to help anchor it, the tree finally came through the windy season without losing its bushy green top.

Many a child stands straight and tall morally because his parents have anchored him against worldly winds. They have taught him God's will for his life as we find it in the Bible. With the Bible as a guide, people are anchored to withstand the strong winds of temptation or adversity.

Jan was a young Christian woman working at a strange new job far away from home. She was tempted, from loneliness, to go out with the wrong crowd. One evening as she was dressing to go out she remembered a Scripture text often quoted by her mother: ". . . think on these things" (Philippians 4:8).

Jan called and broke the date. She went to church instead. There she met the kind of young people with whom she had grown up. Soon she was happy with Christian friends.

*Prayer*: Our Father, help us at all times to realize we are by thy grace made sons and heirs to heaven. Fill us with thy love and spirit. We ask in Christ's name. Amen.

## The Importance of Service

*"Keep thy heart with all diligence; for out of it are the issues of life."* — Proverbs 4:23

Good habits in day-to-day living help make one's life a real success. It is not often that one great, good act performed on the spur of the moment makes a successful life. Successful living involves doing the best you can each and every day.

Happiness comes from a number of things added together to make a pleasant whole. (1) First we must all have something to do. An idle person is never very happy or even nice to have around. (2) Then we need something, or someone, to love. A life lived entirely for self is very empty indeed. Seek for someone to love. It may be a child down the street, a member of your own family, or some unfortunate person in a rescue mission. Love someone. When we are busy, when we love someone, we still need another step to make us truly happy. (3) We need something to look forward to.

All three things may seem to be small things, but they add up to a whole that spells usefulness and contentment. So, develop the habit of feeling that your job is important. Remember that those you love are helped and encouraged by your love. Always look forward to a brighter tomorrow; it might turn out to be the most dramatic day of your life.

*Prayer*: Father, give us sincere and humble purpose as we seek to walk in thy will today. We pray in the name of Jesus. Amen.

## Foxholes and Wonderlands

*"The Lord bless thee, and keep thee: The Lord make his face to shine upon thee, and be gracious unto thee: The Lord lift up his countenance upon thee, and give thee peace."*

— Numbers 6:24-26

Driving down the street I often look at a sign which reads: "A Wonderland of Comfort."

We are all looking for a wonderland of some kind. God has promised that if we follow him he will give us a wonderland of peace.

People who are financially able often build cabins on lakes or in the woods just to have a quiet place where they can get away from the noise and worry of the world. If you are a Christian you do not have to build a retreat away from home. You can learn to retreat into your own mind with happy, pleasant thoughts, knowing who is in charge of your life.

Someone asked President Harry Truman how he managed to carry the heavy load of the last days of World War II. He replied, "I have a foxhole in my mind."

When you feel upset and your load seems unbearable, try entering the wonderland of peace by silently quoting verses of Scripture to yourself. Try thinking of some special blessing God sent you in days gone by. Soon you will be at peace and things will be bright.

One night at church I was almost in tears, just sitting there feeling sorry for myself. A small child went upon the stage to quote some Scripture. She started, "Ask and ye shall receive. . . ."

"You foolish woman," I thought. "You have forgotten to ask." I entered the wonderland of peace and became calm and happy.

*Prayer*: Eternal God, make thy face to shine upon us today. We have been bought with a price; make us ever mindful of our duty as Christians. We ask in the name of Jesus. Amen.

## Facing Life's Problems

*"They were armed with bows, and could use both the right hand and the left in hurling stones and shooting arrows out of a bow. . . ."* — I Chronicles 12:2

Some people practice overcoming the handicaps of life until they are very good at some things. The warriors in our verse of Scripture could use both hands in fighting. In life the person who wins is the one who fails to look at handicaps but determines to fight with both hands.

Lucian Thomas was a businessman who had been hurt in a car wreck during his college days. He loved sports very much, but the wreck left him to live out his days in a wheel chair. Did he quit? No, each year during the football season he would be wheeled out on the playing field to present an award to some worthy boy. He used his quick mind to make money which he would share with a young man in need of a boost.

> If you talk about your troubles
> And tell them o'er and o'er,
> The world will think you like them,
> And proceed to give you more.
> — *Pittsburgh Post*

*Prayer*: Father, let us think of our joys in life. Make our joys like wings to lift us above worldly problems. We ask in the name of Christ. Amen.

## "Whither Have Ye Made a Road?"

*And Achish said, Whither have ye made a road today?*
> — I Samuel 27:10

If at the close of each day someone asked us, "Whither have ye made a road today?" what would be our answer?

Have we put forth an earnest effort to make the way easier for someone in need of help? Have we been cheerful when in the company of those who were sad?

Jesus each day faced a hard road — a road of persecution and trouble. Yet he made the road a brighter and better one for all he touched.

We must never feel that we are a completed person. There always should be the effort to build our lives a little better and a little nearer to God.

> I'm going by the upper road.
> For that still holds the sun:
> I'm climbing through night's pastures
> Where starry rivers run:
> If you should think to seek me
> In my old dark abode,
> You'll find this writing on the door:
> "He's on the Upper Road."

*Prayer*: Eternal Father, give us a missionary spirit. Fill us with joy as we help others along the way. We pray in the name of Christ our Lord. Amen.

## Not Just "for the Birds"

*"The hills melted like wax at the presence of the Lord, at the presence of the Lord of the whole earth."* — Psalm 97:5

There are times when we make a foolish mistake or feel we have blundered. Then we go home and keep going over and over our mistakes and blunders. We repeatedly ask ourselves, Why? Or, we think about some problem we expect to arise, and foolishly imagine all the troubles we will have because of the problems. Such things are making mountains out of molehills. How often people lie awake at night and climb mountains of trouble! On the other hand, when the light of day comes, our mountains often become molehills and are soon forgotten.

We should look at those mountains, those mistakes and blunders, and ask our Heavenly Father to help them melt like wax. Talk them all over with him, then forget them and relax.

> Said the Robin to the Sparrow,
> "I should really like to know
> Why these anxious human beings
> Rush about and worry so."
>
> Said the Sparrow to the Robin,
> "Friend, I think that it must be
> That they have no Heavenly Father
> Such as cares for you and me."
> — Elizabeth Cheney

*Prayer*: Father, receive and bless our lives today. We wish to consecrate ourselves to thee. We ask in the name of Christ. Amen.

## Never Bolt the Door of Tomorrow

*"There is therefore now no condemnation to them which are in Christ Jesus, who walk not after the flesh, but after the Spirit. For the law of the Spirit of life in Christ Jesus hath made me free from the law of sin and death."* — Romans 8:1, 2

Children who are not made to obey authority grow up to be lawbreakers, heart-breakers and burdens to society.

A man I know was an adopted child. As he grew up his parents never corrected him. Others in the family begged them to think what they were doing to themselves and the child, but they resented advice. The boy grew to be a man and he was often in jail, but his father paid his fine and got him out. He married and divorced two wives. He brought children into the world who had to be cared for by others. His parents took the attitude that the world had mistreated him and because of that he was in so much trouble. But actually the parents mistreated him by not making him respect authority from the time they adopted him until he was grown.

"He that spareth his rod hateth his son; but he that loveth him chasteneth him betimes" (Proverbs 13:24).

A good proverb for adults to follow is this: "Never bolt the door of tomorrow by failure to use authority today."

*Prayer*: Father, make us good and worthy parents. We thank thee for our children. Use them, dear Lord, in thy service. Through Christ we pray. Amen.

## Happiness at Your Address

*"Not that I speak in respect of want: for I have learned in whatsoever state I am, therewith to be content."*
— Philippians 4:11

*"Better is little with the fear of the Lord than great treasure and trouble therewith."* — Proverbs 15:16

My friend Julia was ill and cross. Nothing seemed right to her. After a long talk she promised me she would work in her yard for an hour each morning. Soon she was so fascinated with things growing under her care that she forgot to be cross and complaining.

I heard about a man in our city who was laid off from work because of a disability. He got tired of staying in the house and complaining; so he started making doll houses in his garage. Soon he had more orders than he could fill.

Home is the place where we must look for the treasure of contentment and fulfillment. God knew in the beginning that man would need a home and a companion. We often forget how wonderful home is until we have to be away for a long time.

Then we remember, and wish we could relive the days we spent in complaining.

Our homes should be fragrant with the breath of happy events taking place right there, and happy things we plan to do in our own domain.

> Some day I'll stop seeking
> Hillsides far apart,
> When I learn that peace abides
> Only in my heart.
>
> — Edna Becker

*Prayer*: Father, we thank thee for our blessings today. We pray through Jesus. Amen.

## Being Good Stewards

*"Be strong and quit yourselves like men, O ye Philistines, that ye be not servants unto the Hebrews, as they have been to you: quit yourselves like men, and fight."* — I Samuel 4:9

During the depression of the early 1930's, I was a young married woman. Soon I was a young mother with three children. We could have given up the struggle for a livelihood and gone on relief. We chose rather to heed the battle cry, "Conserve every bit of food you can."

Never have I worked so hard and had so many cans of food in my pantry. If some friend had extra beans in the garden we gathered beans. If we had extra milk or butter we helped someone who had none. We are proud of the heritage of thrift and industry we have left our children. We have tried to teach them to be good stewards of what God gives them and to help those in need.

> If any little love of mine
> May make a life the sweeter,
> If any little care of mine
> May make a friend's the fleeter,
> If any lift of mine may ease
> The burden of another,
> God give me love and care and strength
> To help my toiling brother.

*Prayer*: Our Father, we thank thee for giving us enough sunshine to make our pathways gay and happy. We thank thee for enough rain to make us appreciate the good days. May we fight the battle of life like brave men. In Jesus name we pray. Amen.

## Abiding in God's Love

*"He that dwelleth in the secret place of the Most High shall abide under the shadow of the Almighty."* — Psalm 91:1

> No coward soul is mine,
> No trembler in the world's storm-
> troubled sphere.
> I see heaven's glories shine,
> And faith shines equal, arming me
> from fear.
>
> Oh God within my breast,
> Almighty, ever-present Deity!
> Life — that in me has rest,
> As I — undying Life — have power in
> Thee!
>
> — Emily Bronte

A little baby rests comfortably and securely on his mother's breast. A little chicken hides under its mother's wing and is safe from harm. How safe we, as God's children, should feel if we abide under the shadow of the Almighty!

Our problem is not in the power of our refuge, but in our failure to dwell in the secret place of the Most High. His protecting care is ready for our weakness. Let us take refuge there, and abide there.

If we abide in God's love we will find it easier to shut our eyes to the slights and blows of the world upon us. We will be able to say, "I am trusting in God. He will make all things right in his time."

*Prayer:* Father, may we turn our complaints into praise and find joy in thy purpose for our lives. Through Christ we pray. Amen.

## Pilgrims Still

*"Blessed is the man that trusteth in the Lord, and whose hope the Lord is."* — Jeremiah 17:7

Our Pilgrim Fathers are a wonderful example of people who had hope for the future. They had much to fear but they had faith in God. This gave them strength to overcome difficulties and to conquer in a strange land.

God was as near to the Pilgrim band in America as he had been in the homeland. He had as much power as he had in

England or Holland: They had but to trust and ask for help. And they were blessed.

We too have the assurance that if we go forth each day with trust in God he will help us meet our problems. And we will be blessed.

A small child standing on a bench and jumping off to be caught in his father's arms is not at all afraid. He knows his father will catch him and hold him safely. So we too should jump out into life each day without fear, for we with Paul, "Know in whom I have believed and am persuaded he will keep that which I have committed unto him against that day."

*Prayer*: O Blessed Lord, make thy truth to shine about us. Help us to know and understand thy love for us. We pray in the name of the one who was all truth. Amen.

## You Are Somebody

*"And God said, Let us make man in our image, after our likeness: and let them have dominion over the fish of the sea, and over every creeping thing that creepeth upon the earth."*
— Genesis 1:26

What a piece of work is man!
How noble in reason!
How infinite in faculty!
In form and moving how express and admirable!

In action, how like an angel!
In apprehension, how like a god!
The beauty of the world!
The paragon of the animals.

— Shakespeare

You are somebody because you were made in the image of God. Only man was given the breath of God to make his life immortal. Only man was given dominion over the fish of the sea, and over every creeping thing.

What a responsibility! You are somebody, therefore you should act like somebody.

Tom was the only son of a mill owner. His father was very strict with him and always taught him that he was to grow up to take his place in the little town as a leader. While Tom was away in college he was out one night with a girl of doubtful character. When she wanted to go to a place of which Tom knew God would not approve, he seemed to hear his father saying:

"You are somebody; you can't do that." He returned the young woman to her dormitory and never went out with her again. His father's faith in him meant more than the pleasures of a few moments.

*Prayer*: Fill us with a whole-hearted desire to live and act like a Christian should. May the love of Christ constrain us from evil. We ask in Jesus' name. Amen.

## Detour: Life Under Construction

*"It is good for me that I have been afflicted; that I might learn thy statutes."* — Psalm 119:71

Life is sometimes like a highway still under construction — just when a driver leans back and feels all is perfect there is sure to be a detour. We feel all is perfect; the way is smooth; we are happy; we relax. Then adversity strikes and we must go over some rough roads.

Often as we travel the detour we can look across and see the highway. It looks finished and ready for use, and we wonder why it is not open. So in life we have troubles and look back at the good days, and we wonder why we could not have gone on in the same comfortable path. But we must not forget that detours are for our safety.

So also we are safe in the storms God sends us. In fact they are for a purpose. Often the purpose is to bring us into closer fellowship with God; to realize our dependence upon him.

When we are temporarily having trouble and adversity we might remember Milton who, though blind, yet saw Paradise. Beethoven was deaf, yet wrote beautiful harmonies. Adversity is something to be overcome. Contrary winds are to be faced. We can overcome if we put our trust in God. It is good for us to be afflicted so that we may be brought closer to the God we worship.

*Prayer*: Graciously help us to face our trials with peace of mind and faith in thee. We ask in the name of Christ. Amen.

## As Jesus Did

*"How God anointed Jesus of Nazareth with the Holy Ghost and with power: who went about doing good, and healing all that were oppressed of the devil; for God was with him."* — Acts 10:38

Abraham Lincoln used to say he always plucked a thorn and planted a rose wherever he thought a rose would grow.

John Wesley said:

> Do all the good you can,
> By all the means you can,
> In all the ways you can,
> In all the places you can,
> At all the times you can,
> To all the people you can,
> As long as ever you can.

Different people have different ways of doing good but we should all try to live by John Wesley's motto and do all the good we can.

Recently a friend of mine lost her father. As she talked about her loss she kept telling me how many trees her father had planted in his lifetime. "He always said someone would enjoy them." That was his way of making the world a better place.

If you feel despondent and discouraged, go out and do a kind deed for someone. The day will become brighter. This is a cure for blue days. You cannot go far in doing things for others and not feel the love of God reflected in their gratitude. Just giving someone a ride or running an errand may make his day brighter — and yours.

The Scripture says that Jesus went about doing good and then mentions that God was with him. God will be with us if we do all the good we can.

*Prayer*: Give us today a sense of thy presence. Give us a desire to help others. We pray in Jesus' name. Amen.

### Choosing Your Friends Wisely

*"There is a friend that sticketh closer than a brother."*
— Proverbs 18:24

One cannot always choose his surroundings or even his vocation in this world. But one can choose his friends. We should test people's attitudes toward the things which are high and holy before we take them to be our close friends. What kind of influence does a friend have on your life? Does an evening spent with your "friend" make it hard for you to say your bedtime prayers? If that be true, then change friends.

A young man was with a group one night, not knowing how rough and wild they were. Before the evening was over they had robbed a store. The bewildered young man was caught with the group and sent to prison. His life was ruined because he chose the wrong friends for one evening.

There are many faithless friends in this world, but it pays to stay close to the "Friend that sticketh closer than a brother." He will not lead one astray, but will always be there in time of need.

> I am a part of all whom I have met,
> So friend, of me, you are a wholesome part;
> Our precious visits, lingering with me yet,
> Are flowers in the garden of my heart.
>
> — Charles Elmer Chapler

*Prayer*: O Lord Jesus Christ, make us worthy of our friends. Help us always to serve the friend who sticketh closer than a brother. We pray through Christ our Lord. Amen.

## Get Involved!

*"Therefore all things whatsoever ye would that men should do to you, do ye even so to them: for this is the law and the prophets."* — Matthew 7:12

The law of society today seems to be, "Don't get involved." If you stop at a wreck — you may have to take off from work to testify at a trial. If you go to a neighbor's home to help in trouble — you may be sued. So, just don't get involved.

That is not the way Christ would have us live. He said that we should treat others as we would like to be treated. That can only mean becoming involved when we see a case of need. When we see a child being abused, is it too much to notify the authorities? When we see someone needing a boost to get a job, can't we say a helpful word? What if Christ had looked down on a sinful world and said, "I just don't want to get involved"?

If it were not for the fact that some are willing "to get involved" there would be no orphans' homes, no hospitals, no places of charity where the hungry may be fed and clothed. Do get involved. Christ did!

*Prayer*: Father, may we maintain enthusiastic devotion to our task as thy children. May we become so enthusiastic we will strive to be a blessing to others. In thy holy name we pray. Amen.

## Shaken by a Loving God

*"Whose voice then shook the earth: but now he hath promised, saying, Yet once more, I shake not the earth only, but also*

*heaven. And this word, yet once more, signifieth the removing of those things that are shaken, as of things that are made, that those things which cannot be shaken may remain."*
— Hebrews 12:26, 27

Thinking of God shaking the earth and removing those things that are shaken reminds me of a story I heard of a truck driver who parked a large truck in a dry river bed. Since the truck was hard to start he left it running while he went to lunch with some other workers. When he returned the vibrations of the running truck on the quicksand had caused the truck to sink hopelessly into the sand.

We look at the wars and crime going on around us and we feel so hopeless. Yet the last part of verse 27 assures us there are things which cannot be shaken but will remain. There always will be the Word of God—perhaps hidden in our hearts, but we can depend upon it. Jesus will always be near for those who have trust and believe. Because Christ cannot be shaken there always will be love. Christ can understand any language and can be near us in any land.

Perhaps we have been too satisfied with our modern world and God is shaking us up for our own good, to bring us back to a realization of his power and rulership.

*Prayer:* Father, give us the kind of faith which the happiest believers exercise. We pray in the name of Christ. Amen.


## Calling Person-to-Person

*"And he said unto them, When ye pray, say, "Our Father which art in heaven, Hallowed be thy name. Thy kingdom come. Thy will be done, as in heaven, so in earth. Give us day by day our daily bread.*

*And forgive our sins; for we also forgive everyone that is indebted to us. And lead us not into temptation; but deliver us from evil."* — Luke 11:2-4

We made a phone call to our daughter's home twelve hundred miles away. A baby sitter answered the phone. We were so disappointed! We should have called person-to-person. So it is with our prayers, We want to talk person-to-person to our Father in heaven. No one else can do our praying for us. Someone else may pray for our well being, but that will not take the place of our own talk to God about our problems.

These are the gifts I ask of thee,
    Spirit serene —
Strength for the daily task;
Courage to face the road;
Good cheer to help me bear the traveler's load;
And for the hours of rest that come between,
An inward joy in all things heard and seen.

These are the sins I fain would have thee
    take away —
Malice and cold disdain;
Hot anger, sullen hate;
Scorn of the lowly, envy of the great;
And discontent that casts a shadow grey
On all the brightness of a common day.

— Henry Van Dyke

*Prayer*: Dear Lamb of God, we thank thee for all the burdens you have borne for us. We thank thee for the privilege of prayer. We pray in the name of Jesus. Amen.

## Choosing Your Major

*"But seek ye first the kingdom of God, and his righteousness."*
— Matthew 6:33

All through life we are choosing between things we consider to be major and minor. Some people choose to live in what we call major cities; others prefer the small town. Some choose to major on a good education, while to some a good job at the moment seems major.

Housewives will make out a list of things they want to accomplish in a day. Then they will work on what they consider the major items first.

Many college young people start school with one major, then change to another. There is one major in life we should never change. Christ and His kingdom should always be first in our plans and thoughts. If we major on Christ's kingdom the other things in life will just naturally fall in place.

My grandaughter has a puzzle with a cat's face on it. When she works the puzzle she first looks through all the pieces for the face, then she soon has the other parts in place around the face. If we can keep the kingdom of God major in our plans and lives, the minor things will fall into place.

*Prayer*: Father, thou knowest what is in our hearts. Teach us to choose the better thoughts. We pray in Christ's name. Amen.

## "Be Ye Kind"

*"And be ye kind one to another, tenderhearted, forgiving one another, even as God for Christ's sake hath forgiven you."*
— Ephesians 4:32

A little, golden-haired girl passed by a house on the way to the seashore. On the porch sat an elderly man. Often she took time to stop and talk a few moments. Sometimes if she found an interesting seashell, she would give it to the man. Several years went by. Even though she grew older she never forgot to be friendly to the lonely man. One day he died and when his will was read a large amount of money was left for the girl. She had been his only bright spot for a number of years.

We should make a list of things in our hearts that we will remember to do. One should be to treat aged people with kindness. They are often lonely and a kind word is a ray of sunshine.

We should always be ready to make an apology. An apology offered often saves a friendship. After all, God knows who is right or wrong and that is all that matters.

Remember, if you are angry and write a letter, destroy it as quickly as possible. It could carry a poisoned dart.

When someone is starting a scandal and you can do something to stop it, do your best to save a reputation.

You will never regret helping a wayward child find himself. Often he only needs a little understanding and confidence.

You will never regret serving God, and living in such a way as to honor him.

*Prayer*: Father, unto thy name be glory and praise and honor. We offer our love to thee today. In thy holy name we pray. Amen.

## Walking with God

*"The steps of a good man are ordered by the Lord: and he delighteth in his way."* — Psalm 37:23

Abraham Lincoln was born February 12, 1809. He led our country in a wonderful way during the Civil War. The following words were spoken or written by him.

"I am not bound to win, but I am bound to be true. I am not bound to succeed, but I am bound to live up to what light I have. I must stand with anybody that stands right; stand with him while he is right and part with him when he goes wrong.

"I desire so to conduct the affairs of this administration that if at the end, when I come to lay down the reigns of power, I have lost every other friend on earth, I shall at least have one friend left, and that friend shall be down inside of me.

"I have been driven many times to my knees, by the overwhelming conviction that I had nowhere else to go. My own wisdom, and that of all about me, seemed insufficient for that day."

He liveth long who liveth well!
All other life is short and vain;
He liveth longest who can tell
Of living most for heavenly gain.

He liveth long who liveth well!
All else is being flung away;
He liveth longest who can tell
Of true things truly done each day.

— Horatius Bonar

*Prayer*: O Lord, walk with us today. Lead us to serve thee aright. Refresh us and make us better men and women. We ask through Christ, our Lord. Amen.

## Let Hope Drown Out the Thunder

*"For I the Lord thy God will hold thy right hand, saying unto thee, Fear not; I will help thee."* — Isaiah 41:13

Many people live in a state of anxiety all the time. Some are afraid they will lose their jobs or their business. Some women are afraid they will lose their beauty or their husbands. We fear war; we fear robbers; we fear drunk drivers. Parents worry about their children. If one is quiet and likes being at home they try to push him out into society. If a child is too loud they try to quiet him.

This is indeed an age of anxiety. But it need not be if our hope is in the Lord. He has promised to hold our hand and to help us over the trying fears of everyday life.

Let us be done with fear. Why not read the verse above and believe in God's promise? It is better to live in a constant state of hope, expecting the best, than to develop a life of worry.

A little boy once played so loud
That the Thunder, up in a thunder-cloud,

Said, "Since I can't be heard, why, then
I'll never, never thunder again."

*Prayer*: Teach us, our Father, to be kind and patient. Give us power in our lives through love and worship. We ask in the name of Jesus. Amen.

## Love's Supreme Example

*"Greater love hath no man than this, that a man lay down his life for his friends."* — John 15:13

*". . . Having loved his own which were in the world, he loved them unto the end."* — John 13:1

Man is made for love. But there are many shadows and many difficulties in the way of loving and being loved.

When we think of love we usually think of the love of Christ for his redeemed ones. Then we often think next of the love of mother and father for their children, and of children for their parents. We also think of the love of sweethearts—the love of a woman for a man and a man for a woman.

God knew the human need for all these different kinds of love — and gave his blessing to them. He sprinkled love in the hearts of man and woman that the world might be a better place in which to live.

But let us never forget that he made the supreme example of love by giving his Son.

God, give me love; I do not only pray
　　That perfect love may be bestowed on me;
　　But let me feel the lovability
Of every soul I meet along the way.
Tho it be hidden from the light of day.
　　And every eye but Love's, Oh! I would see
　　My brother in the monarch and the bee —
In every spirit clothed in mortal clay.

Give me the gift of loving! I will claim
　　No other blessing from the Lord of Birth,
For he who loves needs no high-sounding name,

Nor power, nor treasure to proclaim his worth;
His soul has lit at Life's immortal flame
A lamp that may illumine all the earth.

— Elsa Barker

*Prayer*: Our Father, the author and giver of all good gifts, look upon us with compassion and forgive our ungratefulness. We ask in the name of Jesus. Amen.

## With Us Always

*"I am not ashamed, for I know whom I have believed and am persuaded that he is able to keep that which I have committed unto him against that day."* — II Timothy 1:12

*". . . And, lo, I am with you alway even unto the end of the world."* — Matthew 28:20

Somewhere there waiteth in this world of ours
For one lone soul another lonely soul,
Each choosing each through all the weary hours
And meeting strangely at one sudden goal,
Then blend they like green leaves with golden flowers,
Into one beautiful and perfect whole;
And life's long night is ended, and the way
Lies open onward to eternal day.

— Edwin Arnold

Even the bravest hearts are sometimes lonely, longing for a companion to hear their troubles and share their sorrows. The gospel of Christ would be empty indeed if it had no message for the lonely people of our world.

Loneliness is like an animal lying in wait in the shadows, ready to jump out and frighten even the bravest. Sometimes it comes because we have lost a dear one, a companion or child. To love is to run the risk of losing. So we all at times go through a lonely period.

But Jesus promised to be with us at all times. He is with us when we are young and look out on the throngs we must meet and associate with to make life a success. He is with us when we are old and feel life is passing us by. He is with us in the thick of the battle, when we feel we are standing alone against a multitude of problems. God is with his children no matter from what vantage point we look at life. We need not be afraid.

*Prayer*: Father, may we keep our hearts with all diligence. Let the beauty of thy love dwell in us. We pray in the name of one **who was always lonely, Christ our Saviour. Amen.**

## Swallowed Up in Victory

*"I am sure that neither death, nor life . . . will be able to separate us from the love of God in Christ Jesus our Lord."*

— Romans 8:38-39

*"So you have sorrow now, but I will see you again and your hearts will rejoice, and no one will take your joy from you."*

— John 16:22

In our work we attend many funerals and see the reaction of many people to loss and grief. One can almost tell how close a person walks with God by his reaction to grief. A strong Christian knows that love stands at the gateway of death and opens the door to a fuller happier life for the one called to go.

"Death is swallowed up in victory" (I Corinthians 15:54).

There is comfort in knowing someone has been relieved of suffering and pain.

True, a house is lonely when a loved one goes away. Jesus knew this would be true so he gave us the promise found in John 16.

> He leaves our hearts all desolate,
>   He plucks our fairest sweetest flowers;
> Transplanted into bliss, they now
>   Adorn immortal bowers.
>
> The bird-like voice, whose joyous tones,
>   Made glad those scenes of sin and strife,
> Sing now an everlasting song,
>   Around the tree of life.

— John L. McCreery

*Prayer*: Father, give us the knowledge today that in thy grace there is sufficiency. We pray through Christ our Lord. Amen.

## Yes, You Can

*"I can do all things through Christ which strengtheneth me."*

— Philippians 4:13

> "I Can't" lacks in nerve; he's too faint of heart
> To pitch in like a man and do his part;
> He has none of the spirit that fights and wins;
> He admits he is beaten before he begins.
>
> "I Can't" sees as mountains what bolder eyes
> Recognize as molehills; ambition dies

And leaves him complaining in helpless wrath
When the first small obstacle blocks his path.

"I Can't" has a notion that, out of spite,
He's being cheated of what's his right.
The men who succeed by hard work and pluck
He envies and sneers at as "fools for luck."

"I Can't" is a loafer, who won't admit
That his life's the mess he has made of it;
The treasure that's sparkling beneath his eye
He thinks he can't reach — and won't even try.

"I Can't" has a feeling the world's in debt
To him for the living he has failed to get.
But, given a chance to collect, he'll rant
About past failures and whine, "I can't."

— Doris Beason

I sat at home for months after a sick spell saying to myself:
"I can't." But at last Mr. "I Can" took hold of my mind, and I
decided to try going out again. Imagine my surprise when my
old friends remembered and seemed glad to see me. Their encouragement and kindness gave me courage to stop hiding behind, "I can't."

We should always encourage people, whatever their problems.
If we believe we can, then half the battle is won. If someone
else says, "You can do it," a lot more of the struggle is won; and
the first thing we know, a victory is won.

*Prayer*: Father, help us to find joy and fellowship in praise to
thee this day. In Christ's name. Amen.

### God's Measureless Love

*"That you being rooted and grounded in love, may have power
to comprehend with all the saints what is the breadth and length
and height and depth, and to know the love of Christ which
surpasses knowledge, that you may be filled with all the fullness
of God."* — Ephesians 3:17-19

When we think of God's love we think of something measure-
less. What a thrill to think of the duration of his love — throughout all eternity, forever and forever! My bank account will run
out and have to be replenished — but not so God's love. Then
there is the width and breadth of God's love. How wide he

made it in John 3:16! It is wide enough to include all who want to be included, from the least to the greatest.

We have different ways of measuring human love but no measuring rod will stretch far enough to measure God's love for his children.

"I love you, Mother," said little John.
Then, forgetting his work, his cap went on.
And he was off to the garden swing,
And left her the water and wood to bring.

"I love you, Mother," said rosy Nell —
"I love you better than tongue can tell";
Then she teased and pouted full half the day,
Till her mother rejoiced when she went to play.

"I love you, Mother," said little Fan;
"Today I'll help you all I can;
How glad I am that school doesn't keep!"
So she rocked the baby till it fell asleep.

Then, stepping softly, she took the broom,
And swept the floor and dusted the room.
Busy and happy all day was she,
Helpful and happy as child could be.

"I love you, Mother," again they said,
Three little children going to bed;
How do you think that mother guessed
Which of them really loved her best?

*Prayer*: Help us to show our love for thee this day as we help others. In Jesus' name we pray. Amen.

## God Is in Control

*"He that hath an ear, let him hear what the Spirit saith unto the churches; To him that overcometh will I give to eat of the tree of life, which is in the midst of the paradise of God."*
— Revelation 2:7

Are you optimistic enough to believe there are better days ahead? If you are, life will be sweet and complaints few. Happy people are the ones who can overcome outer hardships with inner joys.

Sometimes we may feel we are climbing on the rough side of life. But if we are filled with the inner joy of trust in God we will overcome the ups and downs of everyday living. We will then look forward to the joys of life in the paradise God has prepared for us.

I knew a woman whose husband had a heart attack. He lost his job as a result. Then when it looked as if they had no way to go but up, her only son had a nervous breakdown and was hospitalized for months. As a result of the loss of job and financial strain of a long hospital stay they were forced to move out of their spacious home into a small apartment. Through all this the woman, a devout Christian, went right on going to church and kept a radiant smile on her face for the world to see. She knew that God was in control.

> Be it healthy or be it leisure,
> Be it skill we have to give,
> Still in spending it for others
> Christians only really live.

> Not in having nor receiving,
> But in giving, there is bliss;
> He who has no other pleasure
> Ever may rejoice in this.

*Prayer*: Fill us with a yearning for a sweeter communion with thee. We pray in Christ's name. Amen.

## Behind the Scenes

*"And he shall speak great words against the most High, and shall wear out the saints of the most High, and think to change times and laws: and they shall be given into his hand until a time and times and the dividing of time.*

*But the judgment shall sit, and they shall take away his dominion, to consume and to destroy it unto the end."*

—Daniel 7:25, 26

Usually the person who manipulates things behind the scenes does a great deal of work. We think, for example, of the stage hand in a play and the social chairman for an organization. There are many people who work behind the scenes. God is behind the scenes of our life all our days. He understands why some things happen and others fail to happen.

The person behind the scenes is usually rather popular. Men curry his favor because they want his influence. They try to get close to him just to know what is going to happen.

Why then do we so often fail to get close to God? We could

understand the changes in life and meet them better if we were close to the one who is behind the scenes of all things. As the Scripture indicates, sometimes the times are seemingly in the hand of others. But only for a period does God allow Satan to rule. We can be sure that in his time God will take away Satan's dominion.

*Prayer*: May we worship thee with power and understanding. We thank thee Father, for the blessings thou dost shower down upon us. In the name of the great Redeemer we pray. Amen.

## Maturing Beneath God's Hand

*"And ye have forgotten the exhortation which speaketh unto you as unto children, My son, despise not thou the chastening of the Lord, nor faint when thou are rebuked of him: For whom the Lord loveth he chasteneth, and scourgeth every son whom he receiveth."* — Hebrews 12:5, 6

Dare to do right; dare to be true;
You have a work that no other can do.
Do it so kindly, so bravely, so well
Others shall hasten the story to tell.

"I hate to think what that child will be when she grows up." I made that comment as some company with a very unruly child left my home. Not once during all her naughty behavior did her mother correct her and really mean it. I certainly wanted to, but I was not the parent. The privilege should have been hers.

Sometimes it seems pretty rough when we feel God's chastening hand on us; but we emerge better children and more useful to the world. A parent who truly loves his child wants that child to obey certain rules of behavior and thus grow up to be well adjusted in society.

God wants his children to mature by living by a certain set of rules too. We are to be Christlike in all we do. It is easy enough to know what God demands by reading the New Testament.

God is gracious and kind to those who try to live as Christ lived, to those who seek to win others. He gives us many glorious promises if we live by this pattern.

*Prayer*: Father, help us to find thy gracious guidance for our lives. We pray in the name of Jesus Christ. Amen.

## When Your Name Is Mentioned

*"If thou wilt not observe to do all the words of this law that are written in this book, that thou mayest fear this glorious and fearful name, THE LORD THY GOD. . . ."*

— Deuteronomy 28:58

Different names invoke different feelings in us. We honor and worship the name of our God. When the name of The Father of Our Country is mentioned we think with a thoughtful heart of one who left a comfortable home and led hungry men to fight for freedom.

What do men think when your name is mentioned? Do they have pleasant thoughts and feel glad they know you? Or are they cold and unresponsive?

We are the ones who give people the feeling they have about our name. We cannot all be leaders of our country but each of us can fill his own corner in the very best possible way. We cannot all be known far and wide but we can be known by those near at hand as good or bad, as standing for right and wrong.

> Lord of the Universe! shield us and guide us,
> Trusting Thee always, through shadow and sun!
> Thou hast united us, who shall divide us!
> Keep us, O keep us the *many in one!*
> Up with our banner bright,
> Sprinkled with starry light,
> Spread its fair emblems from mountain to shore,
> While through the sounding sky
> Loud rings the Nation's cry, —
> *Union and liberty! One evermore!*

— Oliver Wendell Holmes

*Prayer*: We thank thee, Father, for those great men who have in the years of our history made our nation great. We pray in the name of the greatest of all, our Saviour and Lord. Amen.

## Spending Our Souls Wisely

*"For what shall it profit a man, if he shall gain the whole world, and lose his own soul?"* — Mark 8:36

With a limited amount of money to spend I take my time when I go shopping. I try to make sure I get the full value in my purchases. When I get home and look over what I have bought I like to feel my money was well spent.

As we go through life we have only one soul. We have

only the promise of the present. The past is forever gone; the future is uncertain. Each day we should make sure we spend our time in the most profitable pursuits. Each day is a precious jewel in the chain of our lives and we should get the full value from it.

> Open the door of your hearts, my lads,
> To the angel of Love and Truth
> When the world is full of unnumbered joys,
> In the beautiful dawn of youth.
> Casting aside all things that mar,
> Saying to wrong, Depart!
> To the voices of hope that are calling you
> Open the door of your heart.
>
> — Edward Everett Hale

*Prayer*: O God of truth and holiness, come into our hearts today. Lead us into the better way of life. May we seek and find the pearl of great price. We pray in Jesus Holy name. Amen.

## Petty Pebbles or the Pearl of Great Price

*"Who when he had found one pearl of great price, went and sold all that he had, and bought it." —* Matthew 13:46

Wasn't it fun as children to look for pretty pebbles! (For some of us it still is.) Sometimes we would trade with each other. In our childish hearts we just knew that some day we would find a pebble that would turn out to be a diamond or some other jewel.

Jesus told the story of a man who was searching for something: "Again, the kingdom of heaven is like unto a merchant man, seeking goodly pearls" (Matthew 13:45).

All mankind goes through life seeking something. Some only look for insignificant little pebbles; but others seek a pearl of great price. Some seek financial security; some seek social popularity; some seek fame. All are good, but they are still only as pebbles on the beach compared to the pearl of great price.

A man whose daughter was seriously ill offered the doctor a large sum of money if he would cure her.

"The one who can cure her now demands no money," the doctor told him. "You must pray and ask God to heal her."

How often we let the little, brightly colored pebbles of the world keep us from accepting the pearl of great price! Jesus stands ready to offer us a place in the kingdom if we only accept. We do not have to haggle in a foreign market place as the merchant did. We are offered eternal life as a free gift. Yet many hold out their hand to the world and say, "Fill it with pebbles; the pearl looks too small."

*Prayer*: Give us today true penitence in our hearts. We are ashamed of our negligence and sin. Let us turn to ways of peace. In Christ's name we pray. Amen.

## Making Your Life Count

*"Whatsoever thy hand findeth to do, do it with thy might; for there is no work, nor device, nor knowledge, nor wisdom, in the grave, whither thou goest."* — Ecclesiastes 9:10

How can you make your life count? Begin where you are with what you have today!

We all like to dream of the big things we are going to accomplish some day while we neglect doing the things at hand.

Don't be guilty of saying, "Oh, I am just an inconsequential person."

God made all men important. All have something to do. So our main task is to get busy. As we work at the tasks at hand we find other opportunities opening up for us. We find we can do something a little harder than we thought we could, and we grow.

So you feel small and lost in this vast world? Well, how about a snowflake? Yet we would not want to do without them. They add together and make our winter beautiful; they prepare the soil for the next season. So God has many tasks for the people who may feel they are inconsequential. Put your hand to the task at hand.

> Let us do our work as well,
>     Both the unseen and the seen;
> Make the house where Gods may dwell,
>     Beautiful, entire, and clean.
>
> Else our lives are incomplete,
>     Standing in these walls of Time,
> Broken stairways, where the feet
>     Stumble as they seek to climb.
>
> Build today, then, strong and sure,
>     With a firm and ample base;
> And ascending and secure
>     Shall tomorrow find its place.
>         — Henry Wadsworth Longfellow

*Prayer*: May we be ever conscious that "there is none other name under heaven, that is given among men, wherein ye must be saved." We pray in the name of Jesus. Amen.

## Sometimes "Tomorrow" Never Comes

*"Boast not thyself of tomorrow: for thou knowest not what a day may bring forth."* — Proverbs 27:1

We put off many good things until tomorrow — and then we are sad and disappointed when tomorrow never comes. Today is ours; we should accomplish all the good we can while we have the opportunity.

We often have good intentions for tomorrow. Felix did too. He sent Paul away and thought he would hear more about Christ at a convenient season. That tomorrow never came.

People often fret and lose sleep over problems they expect to arise tomorrow. We fret as if God were not going to be there tomorrow to help us meet our problems and provide a way out for us.

Some parents are so busy they neglect spending time with their children, planning to spend time with them tomorrow. Too often that tomorrow never comes. Before they realize it the children are grown and the happiness of enjoying them as they grow is gone.

Do the things today you have been putting off for tomorrow.

Lord, for tomorrow and its needs I do not pray;
Keep me, my God, from stain of sin just for today.

Let me both diligently work and duly pray;
Let me be kind in word and deed just for today.

Let me in season, Lord, be grave, in season, gay;
Let me be faithful to thy grace just for today.

So for tomorrow and its needs, I do not pray;
But keep me, guide me, love me, Lord, just for today.

*Prayer*: Today let us remember that in thee we live and move and have our being. Renew our spiritual lives. We ask in the name of Jesus. Amen.

## Recipe for Happiness

*"He that findeth his life shall lose it; and he that loseth his life for my sake shall find it."* — Matthew 10:39

The above Scripture is the best recipe for happiness to be

found. As we live for others life becomes worthwhile and we feel whole and complete.

Men are always looking for the radiant life, the joyful life, the truly happy life. Few find it. Those who spend life seeking just what they want for themselves have very little true happiness.

I remember visiting in a beautiful home when I was young. I felt out of place. I was the mother of three small children; my husband was a poor young pastor. The cost of the clothes our hostess wore would have fed us for many weeks. She took us about her house showing off her treasures and accomplishments. I was glad when the time came for us to go. After we left my husband remarked, "What an empty life to have only dishes and silverware to live for."

We can make our lives happy and beautiful by living for others. I know a lady who has no children at home; yet she gives of her time for the small children in her church. She makes the children happy and gives the mothers a few moments rest.

We can be like the Dead Sea, take all we can get for ourselves — and be stagnant and useless. Or we can be like the mighty Mississippi River, giving to all along the way — carrying loads for others. Happiness comes from giving; so we must see how much of ourselves we can give away.

*Prayer*: Father, make our lives beautiful and fruitful. Make us happy in our daily tasks as we serve thee. In the name of Christ we pray. Amen.

### The Touch of the Master's Hand

'Twas battered, scarred, and the auctioneer
Thought it scarcely worth his while
To waste his time on the old violin;
But he held it up with a smile:
"What am I bidden, good people," he cried,
"Who'll start the bidding for me?

A dollar, a dollar, now two. Only two?
Two dollars, and who'll make it three?
Three dollars once, three dollars twice — going for three?"
But no! from the room far back a grey-haired man
Came forward and picked up the bow.
Then wiping the dust from the old violin
And tightening up the strings,

He played a melody pure and sweet —
As sweet as an angel sings.
The music ceased; and the auctioneer,
With a voice that was quiet and low,
Said, "What am I bid for the old violin?"
And he held it up with the bow.
"A thousand dollars? And who'll make it two?
Two thousand! And who'll make it three?
Three thousand once, three thousand twice,
And going — and gone," said he.
The people cheered, but some of them cried,
"We don't quite understand — what changed its worth?"
Swift came the reply: "The touch of a master's hand."
And many a man with life out of tune
And battered and torn with sin,
Is auctioned cheap to a thoughtless crowd,
Much like the old violin.
A mess of pottage, a glass of wine,
A game, and he travels on —
He is going once, and going twice, he's going,and almost gone.
But the Master comes, and the foolish crowd
Never can quite understand
The worth of a soul, and the change that's wrought
By the touch of the Master's hand.
*Prayer*: Touch our lives with thy healing hand. Amen.

## The Rock that Is Higher than I

*"Thou art my rock and my fortress; therefore for thy name's
sake lead me, and guide me."* — Psalm 31:3

There are all kinds of pebbles in the world. There are smooth
round ones, and jagged sharp ones broken from larger rocks.
They may be found almost any place. Some pebbles may be
rubbed and polished; some make nice walks to keep our feet
dry. Some are used to mix with cement and make buildings
and foundations.

For the Christian there is The Rock, Christ Jesus. What a
blessing! What a comfort!

O sometimes the shadows are deep,
   And rough seems the path to the goal,
And sorrows, sometimes how they sweep
   Like tempests down over the soul!

O sometimes how long seems the day,
　　And sometimes how weary my feet;
But toiling in life's dusty way,
　　The Rock's blessed shadow, how sweet!

O near to the Rock let me keep,
　　If blessings or sorrows prevail;
Or climbing the mountain way steep,
　　Or walking the shadowy vale.

Oh then to the Rock let me fly,
　　To the Rock that is higher than I;

— E. Johnson

*Prayer*: Father, Rock of our salvation, guide and lead us in the paths of right. For Christ's sake we pray. Amen.

## I Didn't Mean to Forget

*"For he saith, At an acceptable time I hearkened unto thee, and in a day of salvation did I succor thee: behold, now is the acceptable time; behold, now is the day of salvation."*

— II Corinthians 6:1, 2

When my husband was a boy living on a farm, one of his chores was to get in wood and kindling at night. One morning when his father arose to make the fire, there was no wood and no kindling. The tired boy had forgotten. His father crawled back into his warm bed and called to the son to get up. How cold and dark it was trying to find the wood and kindling in the morning!

"Daddy I didn't mean to forget."

"You didn't mean not to forget either," his father replied.

Many are putting off salvation until a better time. Many will let the time pass and be too late.

There is a tide in the affairs of men,
　　Which, taken at the flood, leads on to fortune;
Omitted, all the voyage of their life
　　Is bound in shallows and in miseries.

— Shakespeare

*Prayer*: Lord of all mankind, ruler of our universe, we ask thee today to give us an urgency in the affairs of the heart. May we trust thee and prepare for the tomorrow of eternity. For the sake of Jesus Christ we pray. Amen.

## It Takes a Sacrifice to Satisfy

*"If thou wilt be perfect, go and sell that thou hast and give to the poor, and thou shalt have treasure in heaven: and come and follow me."* — Matthew 19:20

> Bear on! Our life is not a dream,
> Though often such its mazes seem;
> We were not born for lives of ease,
> Ourselves alone to aid and please.
> To each a daily task is given,
> A labor which shall fit for Heaven;
> When Duty calls, let Love grow warm;
> Amid the sunshine and the storm,
> With Faith life's trials boldly breast,
> And come a conqueror to thy rest.
> Bear on — bear bravely on!

How often as a child I heard the old saying, "It takes a sacrifice to satisfy."

It does take a sacrifice to get the things we want. Jesus told the young ruler he would have to sacrifice earthly riches if he were to have treasure in heaven. Instead, the young ruler foolishly sacrificed eternal life with Christ in order to satisfy his love for money.

A good student sacrifices time he might spend in fun and pleasure, so that he may prepare himself for a life of service. Good parents sacrifice going out too often at night so that they may make a better home for their children. All of life is a choice and we must sacrifice in order to have the best.

Christ sacrificed his life for us. He sacrificed the glories of Heaven for a season in order that we might share Heaven with him. He sacrificed himself for us.

Sometimes Christ does not ask us to go and sell what we have. At times he asks us to give ourselves. He asks us to go and tell the story. He asks us to seek the lost sheep and bring them into the fold. He asks us to comfort the ones in sorrow. Is it too much to spend time for Christ when he did so much for us?

*Prayer:* We thank thee for our assurance of immortality. In the name of Christ we pray. Amen.

## Empty Places

*"And the king sat upon his seat, as at other times, even upon a seat by the wall: and Jonathan arose, and Abner sat by Saul's side, and David's place was empty."* — I Samuel 20:25

David's place was empty because he was afraid of the king. We often leave our places empty in the house of our King, because we are indifferent or lazy.

There is a place in the church for everyone. There is a place of service for all, if it is just to be present to encourage those who lead. How often as a teacher I have felt ready to quit! Then some pupil would express love and gratitude for my work. I started up afresh, ready to work.

Sometimes we attend the services and yet are absent in thought and spirit. How cold the services seem on days like that! We should try never to let our places be empty in the House of God.

> Do thy little; do it well;
> Do what right and reason tell;
> Do what wrong and sorrow claim;
> Conquer sin and cover shame.
> Do thy little, though it be
> Dreariness and drudgery;
> They whom Christ apostles made
> Gathered fragments when he bade.

*Prayer*: Father, may we help all humanity toward the attainment of true brotherhood as we fill the place assigned to us in thy kingdom's work. We ask in the name of Jesus. Amen.

## Traveling Along the Freeway of Sin

*"And now they sin more and more, and have made them molten images of their silver, and idols according to their own understanding, all of it the work of the craftsmen: they say of them, Let the men that sacrifice kiss the calves."* — Hosea 13:2, 3

In some respects the road of sin is like a freeway. Getting on the freeway is much easier than getting off. It is so easy to miss an exit, especially when one is speeding along, hardly conscious of what lies ahead.

The freeway of sin is described in the above Scripture. Once having entered the road of sin, it was easy for Israel to keep going, sinning "more and more."

Occasionally one is forced from a freeway by an accident, perhaps a tragic one, which blocks all oncoming traffic. Sometimes God also uses a tragedy in our lives to steer us from the freeway of sin, back to the narrow road of the Christian life.

The freeway of sin is crowded. Millions are gliding along without realizing where they are going. They sin "more and more." What they do not know is that even though the Christian travels the narrow road, it can be one filled with joy and happiness.

*Prayer*: Everlasting God, who art always ready to hear us when we pray; we thank thee for all thy providential care. May thy Holy Spirit fill our lives and lead us in service for thee. We pray in the name of Christ. Amen.

## Poison Prevention

*"For he that hath, to him shall be given: and he that hath not, from him shall be taken away even that which he hath."*
— Mark 4:25

In the Scripture text Jesus is talking about his followers hearing the gospel and growing in the knowledge of the truth.

In our day we need to be careful what we hear and what we read, for poison can enter our minds and hearts by the wrong speakers and the wrong books.

Bunyan said, "Satan enters in at the ear-gate." But so can truth.

If we lend our ears to false teachers and God-dishonoring speech, we will soon scorn the truth and despise Christian teachings. We will find ourselves drifting off after these wrong teachings, and then after evil companions and deeds. If we love the truth and obey it, our power of understanding will be greater and our knowledge increased. And we will "walk in the truth."

> Lulled in the countless chambers of the brain,
> Our thoughts are linked by many a hidden chain;
> Awake but one, and lo! what myriads rise!
> Each stamps its image as the other flies.
> — Pope

*Prayer*: Give us today a new vision of thy truth. We confess our sin and ask for forgiveness. Create in us a clean heart. In the name of Christ we pray. Amen.

## Have Faith in God

*"And Jesus answering said unto them, Have faith in God."*
— Mark 11:22

Many lives have been saddened because people placed their faith in the wrong people, or the wrong business venture. Many lives have been saved because someone had faith in another and encouraged him. Faith is something unseen, yet having a great influence on people.

A boy was out with the wrong companions one night. As they sat in the car planning to commit a crime he kept hearing his mother say: "Son, I have faith that you will do right."

So he said to the boys, "Let's drive up on the mountain and look down at the lights of the city. The view is just grand from up there. We don't really want someone's old hub caps anyway."

While they were on top of the mountain looking and guessing which lights were where, the boy promised himself he would never be caught out with that crowd again. He did not want to betray his mother's faith in him.

Have faith in God when your pathway is lonely,
He sees and knows all the way you have trod;
Never alone are the least of His children;
Have faith in God, have faith in God.

Have faith in God when your prayers are unanswered,
Your earnest plea He will never forget;
Wait on the Lord, trust His Word and be patient;
Have faith in God, He'll answer yet.

Have faith in God though all else fail about you;
Have faith in God, He provides for His own;
He cannot fail though all kingdoms shall perish,
He rules, He reigns upon His throne.

— B. B. McKinney

*Prayer*: Renew a right spirit within us we pray in the name of our Lord and Saviour Jesus Christ. Amen.

## Work While the Day Remains

*"I must work the works of him that sent me, while it is day: the night cometh, when no man can work."* — John 9:4

When I drive about our city after dark and see the thousands of cars on the streets I often wonder if people know it is dark. The night was designed by God to be a time of rest, and cessation from the toil of the day.

Jesus knew there would come a dark time for him when his work on earth would be finished. He determined to accomplish his purpose before that night came.

We often drift through our days as if we have forever to accomplish the task given us. But we, too, will face a dark time when we can work no more. We should determine each day to work all we can for God, and to pass on the torch of the gospel so that it will keep burning long after we are gone.

If you have not gold and silver
Ever ready to command;
If you cannot t'ward the needy
Reach an ever-open hand;
You can visit the afflicted,
O'er the erring you can weep;
You can be a true disciple
Sitting at the Saviour's feet.

If you cannot be the watchman,
Standing high on Zion's wall,
Pointing out the path to heaven,
Offering life and peace to all;
With your prayers and with your bounties
You can do what Heaven demands,
You can be like faithful Aaron,
Holding up the prophet's hands.

Do not, then, stand idly waiting
For some greater work to do;
Fortune is a lazy goddess —
She will never come to you.
Go and toil in any vineyard,
Do not fear to do or dare;
If you want a field of labor,
You can find it anywhere.

— Ellen H. Gates

*Prayer*: Our Father, we come to thee this happy day and ask that
thou fill our lives with thy presence. For it is in the name of
Jesus our Lord we pray. Amen.

## Starting the Day Out Right

*"And he shall be as the light of the morning, when the sun
riseth, even a morning without clouds; as the tender grass spring-
ing out of the earth by clear shining after rain."*

— II Samuel 23:4

Isn't it wonderful to get up on a spring morning and discover
something beginning to grow in the garden? It fills us with cheer
to see little green shoots peeping out of the ground. We are re-
minded afresh that God is in charge of the world and will make
things right in their season.

Sometimes we miss the beauty of the morning. We begin the
day grumbling or cross. We should be happy and thankful

from the depths of our hearts for the chance of a fresh start each day.

> Some one started the whole day wrong —
>     Was it you?
> Some one robbed the day of its song —
>     Was it you?
> Early this morning some one frowned;
> Some one sulked until others scowled;
> And soon harsh words were passed around —
>     Was it you?
>
> Some one started the day aright —
>     Was it you?
> Some one made it happy and bright —
>     Was it you?
> Early this morning, we are told,
> Some one smiled and all through the day
> This smile encouraged young and old —
>     Was it you?

*Prayer*: Kindle our hearts with love and grace today. May we ever be aware of thy desire to give us bountiful blessings. We pray through the name of Christ. Amen.

## God Expects Something of Us

*"When I was a child, I spake as a child, I understood as a child, I thought as a child: but when I became a man, I put away childish things."* — I Corinthians 13:11

Some people seem to grow up faster than others. I know a fourteen-year-old girl who helps cook, clean house and care for several smaller children.

"Why is she so much more dependable than other girls that age?" a friend asked.

"Because something has been expected of her," was her mother's reply.

God expects His children to grow up and take responsibility. He has lots of work He wants us, as his children, to help accomplish. We should jump right in and try our best to serve. We may make mistakes, people may ridicule us, but with the help of an all-knowing Heavenly Father we cannot fail.

> For life seems so little when life is past,
> And the memories of sorrow flee so fast,

And the woes which were bitter to you and to me,
Shall vanish as raindrops which fall in the sea;
And all that has hurt us shall be made good,
And the puzzles which hindered be understood,

And the long hard march through the wilderness bare
Seems but a day's journey when once we are there.

— Susan Coolidge

*Prayer*: Through this day may the thought of thy nearness to us be in our consciousness. May we be ready to do thy will. We ask in the name of Jesus. Amen.

## Heavenly Light

*"Thy word is a lamp unto my feet, and a light unto my pathway."* — Psalm 119:105

I met a stranger in the night,
Whose lamp had ceased to shine.
I paused and let him light
His lamp from mine.

A tempest sprang up later on
And shook the world about.
And when the wind was gone,
My lamp was out.

But back to me the stranger came —
His lamp was glowing fine!
He held the precious flame,
And lighted mine!

— Lon Woodrum

The Word of God is the greatest lamp we can light for others. The Gideon organization places Bibles in many public places, hotels and motels. The stories they can tell of people who have found God in moments of lonely despair would fill many books. We can all pass on the torch of hope by quoting a Scripture verse, or writing one, to someone.

I knew a man once who was losing his eyesight. He memorized all the Scripture he could each day so that he would still have the light of God's Word when the dark settled down on him. He was an inspiration to others, never complaining, just getting ready. We do not know when there will come a dark time in our life; so we should have a store of memory verses for comfort and strength at all times. We can never give away too many verses of Scripture, for they will always come back to us in time of our own need.

*Prayer*: Make our lives beautiful and fruitful in thy service today. Through Jesus Christ we pray. Amen.

## A Lesson in Living

*"Therefore I say unto you, Take no thought for your life, what ye shall eat, or what ye shall drink; nor yet for your body, what ye shall put on. Is not the life more than meat, and the body than raiment? Behold the fowls of the air: for they sow not, neither do they reap, nor gather into barns; yet your heavenly Father feedeth them. Are ye not much better than they?"*
— Matthew 6:25, 26

Ted was a young business man. He had invested in the stock market and made good. He was very closefisted with his family, and his wife always had to wait a long time for any improvement she wished to have made in the home. One day Ted was stricken with an illness and carried to the hospital. His mother and wife lovingly and faithfully took turns nursing him. As days grew into weeks and weeks into months he despaired of his life. One day he noticed his mother coming in shivering. Her coat was threadbare and she wore no gloves.

"Mother, I am ashamed to have you go cold." He took his check book from the night stand, and as he handed her a check he said, "Take this as payment for some of the many times you have been a free baby sitter for us. Go and buy yourself a good coat and gloves."

Later he also gave his wife a generous check and told her to buy Christmas gifts for the children. She was overjoyed and began to plan for a happy holiday.

When Ted went home after three months in the hospital he was different. His home was a happier place because he started to live every day, not just plan to live for some day when he had conquered the world.

*Prayer*: Let thy grace be our guide and make our hearts living altars of thy love. For Jesus' sake. Amen.

## Searching for Answers

*"This one thing I do, forgetting those things which are behind, and reaching forth unto those things which are before, I press toward the mark for the prize of the high calling of God in Christ Jesus."* — Philippians 3:13, 14

Young people of each generation ask questions about things which bother them. Where did we come from? Why are we here? Where are we going?

The Bible is the source of answers to these questions. Paul tells us that the basic goal in life is getting to know Christ. Other goals become useless and vain when Christ is left out. "Seek ye first the kingdom of God and his righteousness, and all other things will be added unto you." God wants us to pursue that goal willingly.

No one forces us to follow Christ. It is a voluntary goal. His spirit enables us to heed an upward calling. His spirit gives us strength to try for greater things in life.

*Prayer*: O King of all the earth, grant unto us thy blessings this day. Direct our ways in thy service. We ask in the name of Christ our Lord. Amen.

## Two Can Be a Majority

*"The path of the just is as the shining light, that shineth more and more unto the perfect day."* — Proverbs 4:18

Often in life we are faced with a decision between two pathways. If we take one, will it perhaps lead to fame and fortune? Or, if we take a different one, will it perhaps lead to contentment and peace?

A boy about to go overseas to the war front asked his father for advice. The father replied, "Son, always remember two can be a majority as long as one of the two is God."

Often in dangerous places wondering what to do and who to trust, the son would remember his father's statement and he would silently ask his "partner" which pathway to follow.

All pathways lead eventually to life after death. We must choose the path of salvation if we would spend eternity with God.

Which path will you choose?

One is walking with me over life's uneven way,
Constantly supporting me each moment of the day;
How can I be lonely when such fellowship is mine,
With my blessed Lord divine!

— Harold Lillenas

*Prayer*: Bless, we pray thee, our home today. Make us more mindful of thy great blessings. We pray through Jesus. Amen.

## Personal Responsibility

*"But he that knew not, and did commit things worthy of stripes, shall be beaten with few stripes. For unto whomsoever much is given, of him shall be much required: and to whom men have committed much, of him they will ask the more."*

— Luke 12:48

Little Joe wanted a dog very much. "You may have a dog but you will be responsible for taking care of him," his mother told him.

At first Joe was very good about seeing to it that the dog was fed and given all the attention he needed. When the newness wore off he began to neglect the dog. One day the gate was carelessly left open and the dog ran into the street and was killed.

God gives each person something for which he is accountable. We are accountable for our thoughts and our desires; for our money and our children. We are accountable for all of life that God has given to us. When we are tempted to be slow and negligent in making the most of what we have we should remember the verse above.

What, my soul, was thy errand here?
Was it mirth or ease?
Or heaping up dust from year to year?
Nay, none of these.

— Whittier

*Prayer:* Let us work no ill to our neighbor. For Christ's sake. Amen.

## The Warm Fire of Love

*"By this shall all men know that ye are my disciples, if ye have love one to another."* — John 13:35

*"Let love be without dissimulation. Abhor that which is evil; cleave to that which is good. Be kindly affectioned one to another with brotherly love; in honor preferring one another."*

— Romans 12:9, 10

One of the most beautiful things in our world is to see a happy Christian family showing love for each other.

Love wore a threadbare dress of grey
And toiled upon the road all day.

Love wielded pick and carried pack
And bent to heavy loads the back.

Though meager fed and sorely tasked,
One only wage love ever asked —

A child's sweet face to kiss at night,
A woman's smile by candle-light.

Love for others, as Christ wanted us to have, will transfigure and glorify our lives.

A man standing inside a cold house was scraping frost from the window.

"Why scrape the frost away?" another coming in asked.

"So I will be able to see out."

"Build a warm fire in the room and the frost will soon disappear," his companion told him.

When we find our life all frosted over and fail to see our blessings, we need to build a warm fire of love in our hearts.

*Prayer*: As we contemplate the unsearchable riches of Christ's love, may we be thankful and joyful. In his name we pray. Amen.


## The Rewards of Honest Labor

*"For even when we were with you, this we commanded you, that if any would not work, neither should he eat."*

— II Thessalonians 3:10

Each day we read in the newspapers stories of people who do not want to work, to serve, or be of use in the world. At times mobs of people run wild, looting and burning the property of others. They have forgotten that true happiness and contentment comes from honest labor.

People who refused to work were known also in the days of Paul and he gave his solution to the problem: . . . if any would not work, neither should he eat."

In the early days of our country when men had to work long hard hours to build houses and plant crops, the rule of no work, no eat, had to be used again.

Jesus grew up in a carpenter shop. He knew what it was to work. He glorified work by his example.

Parents have an obligation to teach their children to work — to teach children there is joy in work. There is no medicine for the human mind and body like honest work.

The heights of great men reached and kept
Were not attained by sudden flight,
But they, while their companions slept,
Were toiling upward in the night.

*Prayer*: Thank thee, Father, for the ability to work. Reveal to us thy desires for our lives. In Christ's name we pray. Amen.

## Getting Rid of Life's Weeds

*"A good man out of the good treasure of the heart bringeth forth good things: and an evil man out of the evil treasure bringeth forth evil things." —* Matthew 12:35

*". . . Wherefore think ye evil in your hearts?" —* Matthew 9:4

A new family moved into our neighborhood. The house had been vacant for some time and the yard was waist high in weeds from a month of rains. Almost as soon as the moving van had been unloaded, the children, four teen-agers, were out hoeing and pulling weeds. Next day I looked out and their yard was all smooth and ready for planting a lawn.

As people, we often let our hearts get all grown up with weeds of jealously, greed, anger, hate and just general dissatisfaction. We can weed these things out of our hearts by getting busy thinking good thoughts, doing kind deeds for others. Already I have almost forgotten what my new neighbor's yard looked like before they moved in. So we as people need to weed out the ugliness from our hearts and forget it. Others will notice the change too. And so will God.

> I will start anew this morning
> With a higher, fairer creed;
> I will cease to stand complaining
> Of my ruthless neighbor's greed;
> I will cease to sit repining
> While my duty's call is clear;
> I will waste no moment whining
> And my heart shall know no fear.

*Prayer*: Take from our hearts all envy and jealousy. Make us mindful of thy love. Fill our hearts with expectation of better things to come. In Jesus' name we pray. Amen.

## Worshipping Hearts

*"Let the words of my mouth, and the meditation of my heart, be acceptable in thy sight, O Lord, my strength, and my redeemer." —* Psalm 19:14

> A room of quiet,
> A temple of peace,
> The home of faith

Where doubtings cease;
A house of comfort
Where hope is given,
A source of strength
To make earth heaven;
A shrine of worship,
A place to pray —
I found all this
In my church today.

— Lennie Todd<br>(from Decision Magazine)

We should worship God every day. Especially are we blessed when we go to a designated place to worship.

I remember as a small child worshiping in a school building. Yet we were happy with the simple worship service in humble surroundings. We felt very fortunate on the days the minister could be there to break the bread of life. Now I worship each Sunday in a very modern and expensive building. But worship must, and can, come from the heart no matter the time or place.

To worship God we must love him and admire the things which he created. To worship we must give our interest, our enthusiasm, and our wholehearted devotion. Then the place makes little difference.

*Prayer*: Father, bestow upon us strength for our daily tasks. Give us quiet in the midst of tumult. Fill our hearts with hope for a bright future. We ask in the name of Jesus. Amen.

## No Stopping the Clock

*"I returned and saw under the sun, that the race is not to the swift, nor the battle to the strong, neither yet bread to the wise, nor riches to men of understanding, nor yet favor to men of skill; but time and chance happen to them all."* — Ecclesiastes 9:11

Isn't it fascinating to go into a jewelry store and see all the different kinds of time pieces — watches, clocks, and even sundials of all descriptions. Yet no matter how intricate, or how beautiful, all can only number twelve hours for half-a-day.

In Strasbourg Cathedral there is a clock which preaches a sermon each hour. At the first quarter glad Childhood emerges and strikes the bell; at the second quarter rosy Youth comes forth; at the third, sober Manhood lifts his robust arm; and at the last quarter, feeble and decrepit Old Age lifts wearily his hammer to strike. When he has finished, Death lifts his arm and strikes the hour.

Put yourself in one of the four groups. How much time do you have left? No one knows except God. So we should all ask the question, "What am I doing with my life?"

Look at the timekeeper of life. No prayer, no entreaty, no skill of physicians, can stop the clock. We must do the best we can with our lives today.

> Time, like an ever-rolling stream,
> Bears all its sons away.
> — Isaac Watts

*Prayer*: Make us worthy of thy great love. We thank thee for thy unnumbered blessings. In Christ's name. Amen.


## Crowning Christ in Our Lives

*"And when they had platted a crown of thorns, they put it upon his head, and a reed in his right hand: and they bowed the knee before him, and mocked him, saying, Hail, King of the Jews!"* — Matthew 27:29

Each day we crown Christ in our lives. When we are disobedient and selfish we crown him with a crown of thorns. If we worship him and follow his leading we crown him with a crown of glory.

In Matthew 21:9 we read how the multitudes went before Christ and cried out praises to his name. Yet just a few days later they were ready to crucify him.

Do we praise Christ today — and tomorrow crown him with thorns? We must remove from our lives the things which keep us from crowning him Lord of lords and King of kings. He is always ready to forgive us our past mistakes and help us do better in the future.

> The king of a wonderful castle am I,
> It needs constant watching and care;
> To keep it so free from all that's impure,
> That Jesus my temple may share.
>
> I'm a king! I'm a king!
> To rule o'er my life victorious;
> My Savior I'll take, He'll never forsake;
> With Him my triumph is glorious.
> — Emma Virginia Miller

*Prayer*: Father, we need thee through all our days. Hear us as we lift our hearts in prayer to thee. Continue to help us with our problems from day to day. We ask in the name of Christ our Lord. Amen.

## A Pocketful for Future Use

*"Thy word have I hid in mine heart, that I might not sin against thee."* — Psalm 119:11

The young mother smiled as she emptied the pockets of a very dirty pair of blue jeans and prepared them for the washing machine. She found pretty rocks, string, nails and a broken pencil. The little boy doubtless felt he would sooner or later have need of the things he had collected in his pocket.

Think of your life as a pocket. Are you collecting things you will need in the future? Are you storing up strength for the time when trials will come? Can there be anything better to have for future use than verses of God's word memorized and ready to recall when we need help.

Some scraps of song and bits of rhyme,
I have tucked away
In the pockets of time
So a certain feeling of wealth still clings
When they are empty
Of other things.
And with my tears a joy will mingle
As I repeat each rhyme and jingle.
— Bess Foster Smith

*Prayer*: Father, smile on our activities today. Make us successful in our undertakings. We pray in the name of Jesus. Amen.

## Preparing for the Ultimate Adventure

*"Simon Peter said unto him, Lord, whither goest thou? Jesus answered him, Whither I go, thou canst not follow me now; but thou shalt follow me afterwards."* — John 13:36

Life is an adventure! We know not today what tomorrow will bring forth. Life is marvelous in its variety and scope. Life is awesome and at times fearsome.

As we pass through the adventures of every day here we should be ever mindful of the much greater adventure which awaits us after death and spend time preparing for it.

When our family is to take a vacation away from home we spend time in preparation. We anticipate what we will need on the trip and plan to take along things to make our trip happy and successful.

As we prepare for the adventure of all adventures we must above all be sure that we have faith in our Lord Jesus. We must have convictions for right living and we must have love for our fellow man.

> My faith is all a doubtful thing
> Wove on a doubtful loom,
> Until there comes, each showery spring,
> A cherry tree in bloom.
>
> And Christ, who died upon a tree
> That death had stricken bare,
> Comes beautifully back to me
> In blossoms everywhere.
>
> — David Morton

*Prayer*: We beseech thee, that we may improve in our service to thee. Consecrate us anew in thy will. We pray in Jesus' name. Amen.

## God's Garden

*"For, lo, the winter is past, the rain is over and gone; The flowers appear on the earth; the time of the singing of birds is come, and the voice of the turtle is heard in our land; the fig tree putteth forth her green figs, and the vines with the tender grape give a good smell."* — Song of Solomon 2:11, 12, 13

Early this morning I went into my back garden and gathered tomatoes and okra. I admired the pretty red crepe myrtle blooming, and I stopped to smell the fragrant honeysuckle. I pulled a weed that had dared to grow among the ferns.

God's world must be to him somewhat like a spring garden. There are people who sparkle and are a joy to behold, and there are people who just plod along making the wheels of industry and life turn smoothly. Then, sad to say, there are those who are misfits in society. They prey off others and only cause others and themselves sorrow and trouble.

Yet God is constantly caring for his garden. He waters, he plants, he transplants, he thins out, he destroys the wicked — all in his own good time.

> A garden is a lovesome thing.
> God wot!
> Rose plot,

> Fringed pool,
> Ferned grot,
> The veriest school
> Of peace; and yet the fool
> Contends that God is not.
> Not God! In gardens!
> When the eve is cool?
> Nay, but I have a sign;
> 'Tis sure God walks in mine.
>
> — Thomas E. Brown

*Prayer*: Let thy love grow in our hearts as flowers in a garden. We ask in his Holy name. Amen.

## In Perfect Orbit

*"I can of mine own self do nothing: as I hear, I judge: and my judgment is just; because I seek not mine own will, but the will of the Father which has sent me."* — John 5:30

In our space age we read and hear a great deal about being in orbit. Christ pointed out the right orbit for himself and for us when he said, "I seek not mine own will, but the will of the Father."

Sometimes we see people who just cannot seem to get into orbit. They are at outs with all they meet and with whom they try to work. They need Christ. When we, as Christ did, seek to do the will of the Father then other things just naturally work out. I have bowed my head many times at the typewriter and asked God to lead me. In a flash my thought became clearer and I was able to go on working.

Try talking to God all through the day as problems arise, and as occasions for thanksgiving come. You will find yourself in perfect orbit with him for a guide and confidant.

> Does life seem a fret and tangle,
> Has everything gone wrong?
> Are friends a bit disloyal
> And enemies full strong?
> Is there no bright side showing?
> Then — as a sage has said:
> "Just polish up the dark side
> And look at that instead."

*Prayer*: With joyful hearts we yield and dedicate our lives to thee. Use us to thy glory. We pray in the name of Jesus. Amen.

## Washing Our Sins Down the Kitchen Sink

*"Cast away from you all your transgressions, whereby ye have transgressed; and make you a new heart and a new spirit: for why will ye die, O house of Israel?"* — Ezekiel 18:31

One time we moved into a new house and there, nestled quietly in the kitchen sink, was a disposal. I quickly learned how to dispose of all the kitchen garbage. I enjoyed peeling vegetables and fruits for the refuse was quickly gone, down the disposal. How wonderful it would be if people could cast away all the wrong and ugly in their lives and see and feel them no more! There is only one way all our mistakes can be forgiven and forgotten. That is by believing in Jesus Christ and asking him to blot out our mistakes.

*Prayer:* Make us our Father, the tender objects of thy solicitude and care. We are weak, wilt thou make us strong. We ask in the name of Jesus our Lord. Amen.

## Taking Responsibility

*"And now also the axe is laid unto the root of the trees: every tree therefore which bringeth not forth good fruit is hewn down, and cast into the fire."* — Luke 3:9

In the first church my husband ever pastored there was an elderly lady who liked to quote Scripture. At times she would get her Scripture and her proverbs mixed. One day in a testimony meeting she stood and glibly quoted: "Every tub must stand on its own bottom."

After services my husband, who was very young and not trained in "The Art of Winning Friends and Influencing People," told her there was no Scripture such as she had quoted. After a few sessions with a concordance and Bible he failed to convince her and she went right on happily quoting it when she felt someone in the church was not fully aware of his personal responsibility.

We are all responsible for our actions. When the great day of judgment comes each will be asked to give an account of his own life.

"Your task — to build a better world," God said.
    I answered, "How?
This world is such a large, vast place,
    So complicated now!
And I so small and useless am —

There's nothing I can do!"
But God, in all his wisdom, said,
"Just build a better you!"

— Dorothy R. Jones

*Prayer*: May thy will be done in our lives. May we be gracious to those about us who need help. We pray for the sake of Christ. Amen.

## More Than Just Plain Pie

*"Bring ye all the tithes into the storehouse, that there may be meat in mine house, and prove me now herewith, saith the Lord of hosts, if I will not open you the windows of heaven, and pour you out a blessing, that there shall not be room enough to receive it."* — Malachi 3:10

We are all human in the fact that we want more than just the plain pie of everyday living. We want meringue on top. We want as much as our friends have, or maybe a little more.

A little girl was moving. She had not seen the house they were moving to, since it was in a distant city. In her heart she had a dream. She wanted a house with flowers growing in the yard. When they had traveled a long way to the new home she became very eager to get there.

"When the car turned into the driveway at the back there were just flowers and flowers," she told friends later. She had the topping on her pie.

The poet Lowell wrote; "We have a little room in the third story (back), with white curtains trimmed with evergreen, and are as happy as two mortals can be."

If we will just read and heed the Scripture for today we will find we have an abundance of extra blessings poured out upon us.

God has his best things for the few
Who dare to stand the test;
He has his second choice for those
Who will not have his best.

*Prayer*: Open the windows of heaven and pour out upon us thy bountiful blessings, we pray. Grant that we may live closer to thee today. In his name we pray. Amen.

## A Celebration of Deliverance

*"And when he had apprehended him, he put him in prison, and delivered him to four quaternions of soldiers to keep him; intending after Easter to bring him forth to the people."*

— Acts 12:4

The above Scripture is the only place in the Bible where the word Easter is used. The name Easter was given to the Passover time later by the Christians.

The Passover was a Jewish festival celebrating the deliverance of the Israelites from bondage in Egypt. The observance of the Passover, for Jews, begins on the evening of the 14th of Nisan (first month of the religious calender, corresponding to March and April) and lasts seven days.

Easter is our chief Christian celebration. We count it the anniversary of the resurrection of Jesus Christ.

The world cannot bury Christ.
The earth is not deep enough for His tomb;
The clouds are not wide enough for His winding sheet.
He ascends into the heavens,
But the heavens cannot contain Him.
He still lives — in the church which burns unconsumed
   with His love;
In the truth that reflects His image;
In the hearts which burn as He talks with them by the
   way.

*Prayer*: Help us today to lift the burdens of those we meet. May we bring hope to the despairing and joy to the sad. In Jesus' holy name we pray. Amen.

### Memories

*"Remember now thy Creator in the days of thy youth, while the evil days come not, nor the years draw nigh, when thou shalt say, I have no pleasure in them.* — Ecclesiastes 12:1

What a disappointment I felt when I met a former school friend, after many years, and that friend failed to remember me. We had shared many good times together and I could not see how she could have forgotten our girlhood.

How ashamed God must be of his children when they get all involved with the world and forget him! He must be sad many times as he sees us rushing madly after pleasures of the world and neglecting to worship or work for him.

God gave each person a memory. If our memory is filled with good experiences we find them to be a well-spring for a radiant life. Good memories feed the heart and help it glow with joy and satisfaction.

Memories brighten the atmosphere when we are with friends. They inspire us when we are alone and meditating.

"I am a part of all whom I have met"
So, friend of mine, tho' you are far away,
Between us may stretch mountain, plain or sea,
Yet by my side you walk and talk each day,
Because you are a precious part of me.

— Charles Elmer Chapler

The most wonderful thing to remember is our Creator and the great things he has done for us.

*Prayer*: Let grace be our guide today. Write thy will upon our remembrance. Fill our hearts with thy love. In the name of Jesus we pray. Amen.

## Reaching Out Through the Darkness

*"All things are possible to him who believes."* — Mark 9:23
*"But Jesus took him by the hand and lifted him up, and he arose."* — Mark 9:27

The deaf and dumb boy was healed when Jesus took him by the hand. What a wonderful moment in his life that must have been! All of us remember times in life when we have felt very near to God. Some of us have experienced times when we felt a miracle had been performed. We reach out in times of darkness and we find God has reached out to help us.

Mrs. Peter Marshall tells the story of an exceptional hour in her life. When the day came that she and her great preacher husband knew that death had marked him they were sad. After they had gone to bed in their separate twin beds and the lights were out, she was overcome with the prospect of his death and conpulsively reached out her hand through the darkness across the space which separated her from her husband. And, she tells us, as her hand reached out through the darkness, it touched her husband's hand! He was reaching toward her.

No service in itself is small;
None great, though earth it fill;
But that is small that seeks its own,
And great that seeks God's will.

Then hold my hand, most gracious God.
Guide all my goings still;
And let it be my life's one aim,
To know and do thy will.

*Prayer*: Gracious God, we thank thee for all the hours of our lives. May we make them count in thy service. In Jesus' name we pray. Amen.

## Just for the Sake of Helping Others

*"How God anointed Jesus of Nazareth with the Holy Ghost and with power: who went about doing good, and healing all that were oppressed of the devil; for God was with him."*

— Acts 10:38

Jesus has been called "the first philanthropist." Jesus came to earth for a purpose and he sought to accomplish that purpose. He seemed to have one great aim in life: to go about doing good — to redeem the lost world from eternal punishment.

It is human to want a measure of popularity. Some seek this one way and some another. I can think of no better way than to follow Jesus' example and, "go about doing good."

A new man came to our church one time. He had some wealth and he started entertaining the people he felt were most influential and could help him gain popularity. He gave expensive gifts to community leaders. When he failed to become as popular as he expected he complained, "They do not appreciate what I did for them."

Real abiding popularity will come when we go about doing good just for the sake of helping others.

*Prayer*: Father, we adore and praise thy name. We thank thee for sending Christ to make a way of redemption. In his name we pray. Amen.

## Christ Is Risen!

*"He is not here: for he is risen, as he said. Come, see the place where the Lord lay."* — Matthew 28:6

*"And if Christ be not raised, your faith is vain; ye are yet in your sins."* — I Corinthians 15:17

Many years ago a man made a speech against the Christian religion. He felt he had successfully proved that faith in Christ was only a product of the imagination. At the close he asked if anyone wanted to comment on his message.

A young minister arose and went to the platform. He turned and faced the audience. Calmly but firmly and with evident conviction he said, "Brothers and sisters, Christ is risen!"

Out in the audience someone replied, "Verily he is risen."

The meeting closed and the flowery eloquence of the atheist had availed him nothing. Christ is risen. He lives in the hearts of his followers today.

> Low in the grave He lay — Jesus my Saviour!
> Waiting the coming day — Jesus my Lord!
>
> Up from the grave He arose,
> With a mighty triumph o'er His foes;
> He arose a Victor from the dark domain,
> And He lives forever with His saints to reign.
> He arose! He arose! Hallelujah! Christ arose!
>
> — Robert Lowry

*Prayer*: Let us stand today in the glory of our God. Fill our souls with a spirit of gratitude for our many blessings. We pray in the name of Christ our Saviour. Amen.

## In the Strength of the Lord

*"My grace is sufficient for thee; for my strength is made perfect in weakness."* — II Corinthians 12:9

We heard a child scream and rushed out of the house. A strange dog had wandered into the yard and was tumbling our two-year-old daughter on the ground. We did not think of ourselves for a single moment. We rushed to the child and rescued her. We had the strength of ten as we pushed that dog away.

Our Heavenly Father hears when his children call and is quick to answer and protect us from evil.

> If grace were bought, I could not buy;
> If grace were coined, no wealth have I;
> By grace alone I draw my breath,
> Held up from everlasting death;
> Yet, since I know His grace is free,
> I know the Saviour died for me.
>
> — George W. Bethune

*Prayer*: Dear Father, help us to remember today that God never forgets his children. No matter how rough the road, help us to remember to trust in the dark hour. We are grateful for thy grace and strength. In the name of Christ we pray. Amen.

## Close to Christ

*". . . All power is given unto me in heaven and in earth. Go ye therefore, and teach all nations, baptizing them in the name of the Father, and of the Son, and of the Holy Ghost . . . and, lo, I am with you alway, even unto the end of the world."*

— Matthew 28:18, 19, 20

> By nature and by practice far
> How very far from God!
> Yet now by grace brought nigh to Him
> Through faith in Jesus' blood.
>
> So nigh, so very nigh to God,
> I cannot nearer be;
> For in the person of His Son
> I am as near as He.
>
> So dear, so very dear to God,
> More dear I cannot be;
> The love wherewith He loves the Son —
> Such is His love to me.
>
> Why should I ever fearful be,
> Since such a God is mine?
> He watches o'er me night and day
> And tells me "Mine is thine."

We have the promise that Christ is with us alway only if we receive him as Saviour and Lord.

Many people want God to be near when they are in trouble, or in need of his help; yet they do not wish to give him their heart and life in service.

Would you be powerful? Would you be useful? Would you be happy? Then meet the conditions which assure you Christ will be with you, "even unto the end of the world."

*Prayer*: Give us more power today to become servants of thine. We pray in the name of Jesus. Amen.

## More Than a Building

*"And I say also unto thee, That thou art Peter, and upon this rock I will build my church; and the gates of hell shall not prevail against it."* — Matthew 16:18

What do I think of when I say "my church"?

Do I think of a place of brick, mortar, steel and plaster? Yes. But I think also of a quiet place of reverence and meditation, a place where I can go and get away from the world, a place to commune with God. Yes, my church is a place of quietness and peace; but it is much more!

The church is a group of people. It is made up of people who have given their hearts to Christ and are banded together to work to bring in his Kingdom. It is people who have helped to make it grow with money, prayers, labor and love.

My church is the bride of Christ. In Revelation 21:9 we read: ". . . Come hither, I will show thee the bride, the Lamb's wife."

> The Church's one foundation Is Jesus Christ her Lord;
> She is His new creation By Water and the Word;
> From Heav'n He came and sought her To be His holy bride;
> With His own blood He bought her, And for her life He died.
>
> Elect from every nation, Yet one oe'r all the earth,
> Her charter of salvation, One Lord, one faith, one birth;
> One holy name she blesses, Partakes one holy food,
> And to one hope she presses, With ev'ry grace endued.
>
> Yet she on earth hath union With God the three in One,
> And mystic sweet communion With those whose rest is won:
> O happy ones and holy! Lord, give us grace that we,
> Like them, the meek and lowly, On high may dwell with Thee.
>
> — Samuel J. Stone

*Prayer*: Father, we thank thee for a church building in which to worship. We thank thee for an organized church to which we may belong. Truly we wish to dwell in the house of the Lord and inquire after knowledge in his temple. Through Jesus we pray. Amen.

## The Example of a King

*"And David had success in all his undertakings; for the Lord was with him."* — I Samuel 18:14

Real success in life comes only through faith in God. This equipped him for service. Many times we are not willing to pay the price.

David had some characteristics which made him successful, even when the king sent him away on hard missions.

He had no place in his life for revenge. Many people ruin their lives because they want revenge on someone.

Our task as Christians is even greater than the task assigned David. We might follow his example getting ready.

Above all, in tribulation he kept his faith in God. David had a magnanimous spirit. He was also resourceful. As Christians we too often go on year after year in the same old rut. We should think of new ways to witness.

David depended upon God for success. David was filled with humility. Too often we get excited over our own importance. Humility is a mark of greatness.

> Oh, not for more or longer days, dear Lord,
>     My prayer shall be —
> But rather teach me how to use the days
>     Now given me.
>
> I ask not more of pleasure or of joy
>     For this brief while —
> But rather let me for the joys I have
>     Be glad and smile.
>
> I ask not ownership of vast estates
>     Nor piles of gold —
> But make me generous with the little store
>     My hands now hold.
>
> B. Y. Williams

*Prayer*: Dear Lord, the strength of our lives, help us not to be afraid of the world and the evil therein. Let us put our trust completely in thee. In Christ's name we pray. Amen.

### The Sin of Pride

*"Pride goeth before destruction and a haughty spirit before a fall."* — Proverbs 16:18

We say a man has too much pride when he is filled with a feeling of self-importance. Pride is repeatedly and severely condemned by God as a serious sin.

The man too full of pride is an unhappy man. He is sensitive. He imagines people are slighting him. A proud man treasures up fancied injuries. Pride is self-destructive.

I knew a boy who was always pampered by his parents. As a young child he could always get his way if he tried. When he started to school he was a problem to his teachers because he expected to be "it" in all the activities. Often he was deceitful because he thought it would get him the things he wanted. When he was grown he secured a good position but was unable to keep it because he expected too much attention. He drifted from job to job always blaming others for his failure. He went through life an unhappy man.

> He that hath light within his own clear breast
> May sit in the center and enjoy bright days;
> But he that hides a dark soul and foul thoughts,
> Benighted walks under the midday sun;
> Himself is his own dungeon.

— Milton

*Prayer*: Give us patience with all those who need help. If we have wronged anyone accept our repentance and forgive us. We pray in the name of one who could do no wrong. Amen.

## Passing Life's Tests

*"Thou hast proved mine heart; thou hast visited me in the night; thou hast tried me, and shalt find nothing; I am purposed that my mouth shall not transgress."* — Psalm 17:3

To live is to be tested. No man has ever gone through life without some trials and times of testing.

A dear friend of mine worked for the same firm since he was twelve years old. At forty, however, he was discouraged because others were coming into the firm and being promoted ahead of him. Because he loved his work and had a family to support he hesitated to quit and look for other employment.

We have all gone through times when we feel someone else is getting the breaks while we lag behind. What if everyone quit when such times came along? There would be chaos in the business world.

If we contribute to life the best we can each day then when times of testing come we are better able to meet them.

We have a little saying in our family, "A tempest in a teapot, it will soon pass."

When we take the tempest in a teapot attitude we can look over problems better and realize they will soon be past.

> There's only one method of meeting life's test:
> Jes' keep on a strivin' an' hope for the best;
> Don't give up the ship an' quit in dismay;

'Cause hammers are thrown when you'd like a bouquet.
This world would be tiresome we'd all get the blues
If all the folks in it jest held the same views;
So finish your work, show the best of your skill,
Some folks won't like it, but other folks will.

*Prayer*: Walk with us today and help us to avoid the mistakes of yesterday. In Jesus' name we pray. Amen.

## Christ's Collection of Valuable Lamps

*"Let your light so shine before men, that they may see your good works, and glorify your Father which is in heaven."*
— Matthew 5:16

I know a lady who collects antique lamps. She has over four hundred lamps of various descriptions. Some are valuable and some are just common. Some are very pretty and some are ugly and crude. To her they all have a history and a meaning. She would not part with a single one.

We are Christ's lamps. He commissioned us to shine before the world and point men to him. If we are followers of Christ we must make our presence felt by letting our Christian light shine.

His lamp am I, to shine where He shall say;
And lamps are not for sunny rooms,
Nor for the light of day;
But for dark places of the earth;
Where shame, and crime and wrong have birth;
Or for the murky twilight gray
Where wandering sheep have gone astray;
Or where the light of faith grows dim,
And souls are groping after Him . . .
So may I shine — His light the flame —
That men may glorify His name.

*Prayer*: Dear Lord, our light and our salvation, strengthen our lives today. May we seek after thee and be conscious of thy presence. In the name of our Lord Jesus we pray. Amen.

## The Blessings of Charity

*"And above all things have fervent charity among yourselves; for charity shall cover the multitude of sins."* — I Peter 4:8

In my Mission Society meeting an appeal was read from a college student for help. He wanted empty cartons, pretty bottles, crayons. He was working in the very poorest part of town and he wanted to help the children make Christmas gifts out of our discarded things. At the very bottom of his letter he stated, "It would be so nice if we could have enough money to buy each child an apple."

Almost everyone in the meeting put in a generous offering toward purchase of the apples. We could enjoy our own feast if we had helped those children have a little treat.

I gave my life for thee, My precious blood I shed,
That thou might'st ransomed be. And quickened from the dead;
I gave my life for thee, what hast thou given for me?

> My Father's house of light, My glory circled throne,
> I left for earthly night, For wanderings sad and lone;
> I left it all for thee, Hast thou left aught for me?

> I suffered much for thee, more than thy tongue can tell,
> Of bitterest agony, To rescue thee from hell;
> I've borne it all for thee, What hast thou born for me?

> And I have brought to thee, Down from my home above,
> Salvation full and free, My pardon and my love;
> I bring rich gifts to thee, What hast thou brought to me?

> — Frances Havergal

*Prayer*: O God, the Father of lights, from whom cometh every good and perfect gift, help us to be generous to those less fortunate than ourselves. For the sake of Christ our Saviour we pray. Amen.

## The Bread of Life

*"I am the bread of life; he who comes to me shall not hunger and he who believes in me shall never thirst."* — John 6:35

We all recognize the need for physical food. We will work long hours for small pay, if necessary, in order to buy food. Few of us realize the necessity for spiritual food.

Jesus said, "I am the bread of life." He becomes our bread of life when we believe in him as our personal Saviour and Lord.

Sometimes people do not have enough physical food to divide with a needy friend or brother. This is never true with spiritual food. The more we share it with others the richer and fuller our own lives become.

A small child was converted one night in a revival service. The father of the child was not a Christian, but he was at the services that night. After the child felt the cleansing love of Christ she turned away from the altar and went to her father. She did not say a word, but just took his hand and gently led him to the altar. To have the bread of life is to want to share it with others.

> Break Thou the bread of life, dear Lord, to me,
> As Thou didst break the loaves beside the sea;
> Beyond the sacred page I seek Thee Lord;
> My spirit pants for Thee, O living Word.

> — Mary Ann Lathbury

*Prayer*: Father, help us to place our hand in thine and walk in faith this day. Help us always to believe that all things work for good to thy children. In Christ's name we pray. Amen.

## Dying to Live

*"He who loves his life loses it, and he who hates his life in the world will keep it for eternal life."* — John 12:25

A story came to us from the Vietnam war of a young soldier who threw himself upon a grenade in order to save his men. He literally gave his life for the men with him.

Jesus sought to make his followers realize that to serve God they were to give their lives in service for others.

Many times Jesus stated the principle of dying to live. The only way we can be fruitful is by giving up our lives in service.

> Must Jesus bear the cross alone,
> And all the world go free?
> No: there's a cross for everyone.
> And there's a cross for me.

> The consecrated cross I'll bear,
> Till death shall set me free;
> And then go home my crown to wear,
> For there's a crown for me.

> — Thomas Shepherd

If a grain of wheat fall into the ground it will live again — and bring forth fruit.

*Prayer*: Father, we direct our prayer to thee today and look up to thee for guidance. Bless our loved ones and make them happy. We ask in the name of Jesus. Amen.

## On Business for My King

*"Now then we are ambassadors for Christ, as though God did beseech you by us: we pray you in Christ's stead, be ye reconciled to God."* — II Corinthians 5:20

When I was a child my mother often sent me on errands. I was really an ambassador for my mother. As a wife I am, at times, an ambassador for my husband when he cannot attend some meeting. My most important place as an ambassador is to be an ambassador for Christ, to tell the story of salvation to those who do not know His love.

I am a stranger here, within a foreign land;
My home is far away, upon a golden strand;
Ambassador to be of realms beyond the sea,
    I'm here on business for my King.

My home is brighter far than Sharon's rosy plain,
Eternal life and joy thro'-out its vast domain;
My Sov'reign bids me tell how mortals there may dwell,
    And that's my business for my King.

This is the message that I bring,
A message angels fain would sing:
"Oh, be ye reconciled,"
Thus said my Lord and King,
    "Oh, be ye reconciled to God."

               — E. T. Cassel

*Prayer*: Father, make us worthy ambassadors in thy service. We offer this petition in the name of Jesus. Amen.

## Living for Today

*"Sufficient unto the day is the evil thereof."* — Matthew 6:34

*"Thy shoes shall be iron and brass; and as thy days, so shall thy strength be."* — Deuteronomy 33:25

We should not be burdened today with the past. We should cast all our past cares upon God who forgives our sins. And then we should confidently and courageously press on to the future.

Our anxiety today cannot change our tomorrow. So why fret. Let us commit our ways unto the Lord and live as abundantly as possible today.

      Could we but lift tomorrow's veil
        And read there all our trouble,

Today's sweet joys would fade away,
   And all our sorrows double.

We'll have enough of pain today,
   Don't look ahead to borrow.
For God has hung a friendly veil
   Between us and tomorrow.

Yes, God has kindly hid from us
   Each pain or heavy trial,
And bids us trust to Him alone,
   Each joy or self-denial.

"Give us this day our daily bread,"
   Then crave not more, my brother:
Be thankful for the loaf you have,
   And then He'll give another.
                              — D. Y. Bagby

*Prayer*: Father, we praise thee for all thy mercies. Fellowship with thee brings us so much joy and so many blessings. Through Jesus Christ we pray. Amen.

## No Strife Between Us

*"And Abram said unto Lot, Let there be no strife, I pray thee, between me and thee, and between my herdmen and thy herdmen; for we be brethren."* — Genesis 13:8

How sweet it is to visit in a home where the children play happily together, and where the mother and father show love and affection for each other.

There is beauty all around,
When there's love at home;
There is joy in every sound,
   When there's love at home.
Peace and plenty here abide,
Smiling sweet on every side,
Time doth softly, sweetly glide,
   When there's love at home.

A large family I know has one child with bad eyes. As a consequence she often stumbles and is very hard on her shoes. When she has to have shoes before the others they do not act jealous. They smile and say, "Sister is harder on her shoes than the rest of us."

Right-thinking people want home to be a foretaste of heaven.

That can only be accomplished by all the members in a family loving each other; by all members of a family thinking of others first.

*Prayer*: Grant us the ability to face life's tasks with joyful hearts. May we earnestly endeavor to live in peace and harmony with those round about us. In Christ's name we pray. Amen.

## What Will I Do with My Heart?

*"Give me thine heart."* — Proverbs 23:26

"Give me thy heart," says the Father above,
No gift so precious to him as our love,
Softly he whispers wherever thou art,
"Gratefully trust me, and give me thy heart."

Every living person has a precious gift to bestow on someone or something. It is the gift of his heart! Young people look for a worthy lover to whom they may give their heart. Older people often bestow their hearts upon a cause. We must have something upon which to bestow our affections.

The heart is a precious gift. Christ gave his all on Calvary in order to make our hearts pure. We owe our hearts to Christ because of his divine grace.

A professional juggler was seen one day at the altar of the church juggling a handful of balls.

"Why are you doing this in the church?" the pastor asked.

"This is what I know how to do and I want to dedicate my talent to God."

The juggler went out to give free shows to the sick in the city's hospitals.

It is my choice to make. What will I do with my heart, my most precious gift? Will I give it to the Lord or to the world?

*Prayer*: In everything we give thanks to thee. May we today give our hearts and lives to thee. For Jesus' sake we pray. Amen.

## Showing Mercy

*"Therefore they gathered them together, and filled twelve baskets with fragments of the five barley loaves, which remained over and above unto them that had eaten."* — John 6:13

Jesus saw the multitude of people and knew they were very hungry. His heart was touched in such a way that he performed a miracle. He did not provide just enough bread and fish to give each one a taste. There was enough for all to be filled, and then there were twelve baskets full left over.

God treats us just this way every day. He gives us so many blessings we always have enough and to spare.

Do we show the same mercy to our fellow man as we expect God to show towards us? What if God forgave our sins in the same way we forgive others? What if God provided for us in the same way we provide for those in need? We expect him to be so merciful to us and often forget to show mercy to those about us.

> There's a wideness in God's mercy,
>     Like the wideness of the sea;
> There's a kindness in his justice,
>     Which is more than liberty.
>
> For the love of God is broader
>     Than the measure of man's mind,
> And the heart of the Eternal
>     Is most wonderfully kind.

*Prayer*: Our heavenly Father, help us today to remember our Saviour Jesus Christ and the great gift he made for us. Cleanse us and make us worthy. We ask in the name of Jesus. Amen.

## The Secret of a Happy Life

"*. . . she remembereth not her last end; therefore she came down wonderfully: she had no comforter.*" — Lamentations 1:9

In our Scripture verse the writer was talking about the city of Jerusalem, and the fact that the pleasures of the day had blotted out the thoughts that there would be a time of reckoning in the future.

We should not have as our aim in life only animal indulgence in the day at hand. Neither should we live only for what we hope to gain tomorrow. To be happy we must have a high aim in life, and seek to enjoy each day as we work to accomplish our aim.

An artist painting a picture sees the finished picture in his mind's eye before he puts the first color on the canvas. Yet he enjoys the work of painting and the ultimate finishing of the picture.

Psalm 16:8 reads, "I have set the Lord always before." This verse is the secret of a successful and happy life. It will give us the enthusiasm to enjoy today and the desire to prepare for to-morrow.

*Prayer*: Clothe us with thy righteousness and give us joy as thy children today. In his name we pray. Amen.

## Just Browsing

*"And if it seem evil unto you to serve the Lord, choose you this day whom ye will serve . . . but as for me and my house, we will serve the Lord."* — Joshua 24:15

Mary was in a large department store when a friend came rushing by. "Hello, Mary, what are you doing?"

"Oh, I am just browsing," was Mary's reply.

I saw Mary in the library and asked the same question. I received the same pat answer: "Oh, I am just browsing."

Some people develop the habit of just browsing through life with no real purpose in mind.

Life spent merely in browsing is wasted. We must choose whom we will serve and then work with a will to accomplish that service.

> Give us great dreams, O God, while Thou art giving,
>     And keep the end; it is enough if we
> Live by the hope, nor falter in the living,
>     That lures us on from dust to dignity.
>
> Give us the courage of the soul's high vision,
>     Though its fulfillment here we never see;
> The heart to make and keep the brave decision,
>     And faith to leave the ultimate with Thee.

— Marie Le Nart

*Prayer*: Lord, help me to make the most of every day. Let me not waste the precious moments of life in wandering like a butterfly from leaf to leaf. May my purpose be a noble one. Give me grace to accomplish it. Amen.

## Give of Yourself

*"Freely ye have received, freely give."* — Matthew 10:8

*"Give, and it shall be given unto you; good measure, pressed down, and shaken together, and running over, shall men give into your bosom. For with the same measure that ye mete withal it shall be measured to you again."* — Luke 6:38

Give plenty of what is given to you,
      Listen to pity's call;
Don't think the little you give is great,
      And the much you get is small.

— Phoebe Cary

Two men gave large gifts to an orphanage in our city. One of the men went to the office of the superintendent and sat for a few moments chatting before he left his check. None of the children saw him or heard of his gift.

The other man filled his pockets with quarters and went to the home when the children were outside playing. He gave each child a piece of money, a kind word and a loving pat or hug. As he was about to leave he dropped by the main office and left a check.

Both men gave liberally but one also gave a little bit of himself to each child.

We too must be sure that as we give to worthy causes in life we do not neglect also to give of ourselves.

Put a song in someone's heart and you will find a song in your own.

*Prayer*: Father, we are rich in thy mercy. May we today share with someone in need. In the name of Christ we pray. Amen.

## Forget the Trifles

*"When I was a child, I spake as a child, I understood as a child, I thought as a child: but when I became a man I put away childish things."* — I Corinthians 13:11

"Don't fuss about trifles. Don't permit little things — the mere termites of life — to ruin your happiness" (from the writings of Dale Carnegie).

Joy was a pretty girl with a happy name — but she was not happy. Always she was bothered about the little trifles of life. She could not enjoy a picnic because her hair might blow out of place. She could not relax at school if she failed to get time to refresh her makeup between classes. Her life was just a miserable story of little bothers.

Tom, Joy's brother, was ugly and freckled but he was happy in life. He knew what he hoped to achieve in school and he never worried when some little things went wrong. He just thought about his goal and pressed on.

If a wren can cling
To a spray a-swing
In the mad May wind, and sing and sing,
As if she'd burst for joy;
Why cannot I
Contented lie
In His quiet arms beneath the sky,
Unmoved by earth's annoy?

— F. B. Meyer

*Prayer*: Help us today to be thoughtful of others. Give us an opportunity to show thy love to someone. We ask in the name of Jesus. Amen.

## The Gospel of Love

*"And to love him with all the heart, and with all the understanding, and with all the soul, and with all the strength, and to love his neighbor as himself, is more than all whole burnt offerings and sacrifices."* — Mark 12:33

The gospel of love has built hospitals, orphans' homes, schools and many other worthy things too numerous to mention.

Love makes a home happy and lack of love causes homes to break apart. A popular little chorus ran as follows:

It's love, it's love
It's love that makes the world go 'round
It's love, it's love
It's love that makes the world go 'round.

A boy twelve years old saved his allowance and bought a long bicycle seat.

"Why get that type seat when you had a good one?" asked his buddy.

"So I can ride my baby sister in front of me," was his reply.

He loved his little sister so much he wanted her to share his fun.

We enjoy many things because we are Christians. Our nation is better because Christians love and want to share the gospel story.

We've a story to tell to the nations,
That shall turn their hearts to the right,
A story of truth and sweetness,
A story of peace and light,
A story of peace and light.

For the darkness shall turn to dawning,
And the dawning to noon-day bright,
And Christ's great kingdom shall come on earth,
The kingdom of love and light.

— Colin Sterne

*Prayer*: May we spend this day rejoicing in thy love. In Jesus
name we pray. Amen.

## Quenching Our Thirst Forever

*"And the Spirit and the bride say, Come. And let him that
heareth say, Come. And let him that is athirst come. And
whosoever will, let him take the water of life freely."*

— Revelation 22:17

One summer I picked cotton on a farm in Texas. I weighed
less than a hundred pounds and I hated the sun. But I needed
the clothes I could buy with the money. Those were the longest
rows in the world! I would get so thirsty during the long afternoon. One day when we were just about to finish a bale, the
farmer's wife came to the field, and brought some cold lemonade.
How refreshing it was!

We are often thirsty and tired in this life. Christ offers us
the refreshing water of life, freely.

High in the Father's house above
    My mansion is prepared;
There is the home, the rest I love.
    And there my bright reward.

With Him I live, in spotless white,
    In glory I shall shine;
His blissful presence my delight,
    His love and glory mine.

All taint of sin shall be removed,
    All evil done away;
And I shall dwell with God's Beloved
    Through God's eternal day.

*Prayer*: Our Father, who sits upon the throne, help us to be
prepared for the day when thou shalt come to make all things
new. In the name of Christ we pray. Amen.

## Fighting to Win the World

*"Go ye therefore, and teach all nations, baptizing them in the name of the Father, and of the Son, and of the Holy Ghost: Teaching them to observe all things whatsoever I have commanded you: and, lo, I am with you alway, even unto the end of the world."* — Matthew 28:19, 20

When Japan attacked our country at the beginning of World War II, many men rushed to the recruiting offices all over our country. Our country was in great danger and they were eager to fight for the cause of freedom. Twenty odd years later we found ourselves in a war for which we had little stomach. Men were sent to Vietnam for a cause not clear to many Americans. Some refused to go; others who went were bitter. And the end of it all? Many Americans want to forget the whole affair.

Christ left us instructions and orders to fight for the supreme cause of winning the lost world to the cause of Christianity. Are we rushing to obey his orders?

Who can surrender to Christ, dividing his best with the
stranger,
Giving to each what he asks, braving the uttermost danger
All for the enemy, Man? Who can surrender till death
His words and his works, his house and his lands,
His eyes and his heart and his breath?
Who can surrender to Christ? Where is the man so trans-
cendent,
So heated with love of his kind, so filled with the spirit
resplendent
That all of the hours of his day his song is thrilling and
tender,
And all of his thoughts to our white cause of peace Sur-
render, surrender, surrender?

— Vachel Lindsay

*Prayer*: Father, make us diligent to fight for the cause of Christ, our Lord. Give us courage always to stand for the right. In the name of Jesus we pray. Amen.

## Flowers that Last Forever

*"The grass withereth, the flower fadeth: but the word of our God shall stand forever."* — Isaiah 40:8

A thing of beauty is a joy for ever:
Its loveliness increases; it will never
Pass into nothingness.

— John Keats

Little Joe brought a handful of wild flowers to his mother. She tenderly put them in a glass of water. In spite of water and care they were gone in a few days.

"Why do beautiful things have to fade away?" Joe asked his mother.

"They are not entirely gone," answered his mother. "I will always remember how sweet my little boy was to bring me some flowers."

Kind words and deeds keep right on living even when we cannot see their symbols anymore.

*Prayer*: We give thanks for thy loving care in days past. In the name of Jesus we pray. Amen.

## The Importance of a Good Name

*"A good name is rather to be chosen than great riches, and loving favor rather than silver and gold."* — Proverbs 22:1

Who steals my purse steals trash; 'tis something, nothing;
'Twas mine, 'tis his, and has been slave to thousands;
But he that filches from me my good name
Robs me of that which not enriches him,
And makes me poor indeed.

— William Shakespeare

When James was a young boy he often thought his father was old fashioned. At times he resented not being able to live in a more modern manner. One day he left home and went out to make his own way in the world. He tried hard to find a job but times were hard and he had no luck. Almost out of funds, tired and discouraged he came to the home of a man his father had told him about.

"Son, I will help you get a job. I admire your father, and you would have to be a good boy to be his son."

So the two together went to look for a job, and soon the boy was hired because of his father's good name.

I heard of another young man many years later when times were good, who had difficulty getting work in his community because his father was a drunkard. Often the boy was made to suffer because the name he wore was not one of which he could be proud.

We can all work for a good name. What about your name?

*Prayer*: Help us in times of stress to remember our good name and keep it pure. In Christ's name we pray. Amen.

## Faith in Our Father

*"For I know whom I have believed and am persuaded that he is able to keep that which I have committed unto him against that day."* — II Timothy 1:12

Most children have faith in their parents. They seem instinctively to feel that father and mother will provide for them. Should we not trust our Heavenly Father?

A ten-year-old boy living far out in the country helped his father cut and load a cord of wood. "I will take the wood to town and sell it. Then I will buy some gifts for the family," the father promised.

The father spent the entire day driving to town and up and down the streets trying to sell the wood. At last when dark had almost settled he was successful in making a sale. All the stores were closed and he made the long drive home without any gifts.

"The children stayed up until they were exhausted waiting for you to return," his wife told him.

"What will I do?" he asked her. "The stores were all closed by the time I sold the wood."

"Give each of them a piece of money and on Saturday we will all go to town and buy something," his wife advised.

How pleased the children were with their coins and the prospect of a trip to town! Going to town seemed much nicer than just a gift brought home.

Sometimes we fear our Heavenly Father has forgotten us, but he always has a better gift in store for us than we expected.

*Prayer*: May we think today on things that are Christ-like. We pray in the name of Jesus. Amen.

## The Abundant Life

*"The thief cometh not, but for to steal, and to kill, and to destroy: I am come that they might have life, and that they might have it more abundantly."* — John 10:10

"Life is made up, not of great sacrifices or duties, but of little things, in which smiles and kindnesses and small obligations, given habitually, are what win and preserve the heart and secure comfort" (Sir Humphry Davy).

Christ wants us to have life more abundantly; yet he did not at any time advise people to seek for glory, fame, or fortune. He wants us to have a more abundant life; yet he did not set an example of extravagant living.

What is an abundant life? It is one filled with serenity and peace. We can have serenity by putting our lives in his care. We can have peace by seeking to follow his will.

The man and woman who close their door on the world at night and enjoy fellowship with their own children are happy indeed. So also is life with Christ.

> Into my heart's treasury
> I slipped a coin
> That time cannot take
> Nor a thief purloin, —
> Oh, better than the minting
> Of a gold-crowned king
> Is the safe-kept memory
> Of a lovely thing.
>
> — Sara Teasdale

*Prayer*: May we have a larger life by thinking on lovely things. Keep us from being impatient and irritable today. We pray through the name of Jesus. Amen.

## Restrictions Make the Difference

*"For whom the Lord loveth he chasteneth, and scourgeth every son whom he receiveth. If ye endure chastening, God dealeth with you as with sons; for what son is he whom the father chasteneth not? — Hebrews 12:6, 7*

Is there anyone or anything you despise more than a child or pet that is never restricted in any way? If people are to be agreeable and pleasant, they must live by some restrictions.

Two boys lived on the same block. Tim was required to go to bed at eight-thirty on school nights. Brady was not required to go to bed at all unless he wanted to. Brady's parents often wondered why Tim made such good grades — why he was so good in sports — why he grew up to be so popular. They could not understand why their son did not accomplish as much as Tim and why he never received so much as a kind word from his teachers. Restrictions made the difference!

We must all learn to live by life's restrictions. We cannot say "yes" to every request, every whim.

> All that we say returns,
> The bitter word or sweet;
> Days, weeks, or years may intervene,
> But soon or late
> The spoken word and speaker meet.

> All that we do returns:
> The deed that's true or base
> We may forget, but all unseen
> And parallel
> The doer and the deed keep pace.
> — John Richard Moreland

*Prayer*: Father, if temptation assails us today, give us strength to resist it. If trouble comes our way give us courage to face it. We pray in the name of one who faced both temptation and trouble. Amen.

## Refreshing Showers

*"And I will make them and the places round about my hill a blessing; and I will cause the shower to come down in his season: there shall be showers of blessing."* — Ezekiel 34:26

Before the days of air-conditioned cars a family stopped at our house on a hot summer day. They had traveled several hundred miles and were so exhausted from the heat that the mother had to go to bed for a while.

After visiting for an hour our friends felt they must press on toward their destination. How we hated to see them start out in the heat again! As we stood by the car bidding them goodbye a cloud came over the sun. In a few moments they drove away in a shower of rain. We were so glad that they would be cooled and refreshed as they traveled.

When life seems unbearably hard and we think it is impossible to go on, God often sends a refreshing shower. Sometimes it is merely a word of encouragement from a friend.

> Who loves the rain
> And loves his home,
> And looks on life with quiet eyes,
> Him will I follow through the storm;
> And at his hearth-fire keep me warm;
> Nor hell nor heaven shall that soul surprise,

Who loves the rain,
And loves his home,
And looks on life with quiet eyes.
— Frances Shaw

*Prayer*: Father, we would begin the day aright with worship. We feel refreshed and renewed from our rest of the night. We ask thee to guide us today. In the name of Jesus we pray. Amen.

## Our Sure Source of Comfort

*"O thou that hearest prayer, unto thee shall all flesh come."*
— Psalm 65:2

Oh how I need a friend today,
To help me o'er life's rugged way.
There is a friend who cares, I say,
The one who hears me when I pray,
Who knows each idle word I say.
He climbed a rough high hill one day
That I might have the right to pray.
— Amy Bolding

There comes a time in every life when we have only one source of comfort. We should be very careful to keep the line open at all times to our God, the source of our comfort and strength.

That I may grow a little braver
To face life's trials and never waver
From high ideals that I have made,
To face life squarely, unafraid.
That I may yet more patient be
With those, who faltering lean on me.
To profit by mistakes I've made
And let them from my memory fade.
That I may always faithful be
To those who put their trust in me.
For these, dear, heavenly Lord,
I pray that I may prove worthwhile today!

*Prayer*: O Lord, help us to be honest in dealing with ourselves, as we expect others to be when they deal with us. May we realize that if we cheat in life, we hurt ourselves most of all. Make us willing to accept thy Lordship over us. Grant us power to live for thee regardless of hardship or trial. We pray for the sake of one who gave all for us, Jesus our Saviour. Amen.

## Working as He Worked

*"So God created man in his own image."* — Genesis 1:27
*"But Jesus answered them, My Father worketh hitherto, and I work."* — John 5:17

Little Johnny was out working on his wagon. He was attempting to change the wheels.

"Why are you tearing up your wagon?" a neighbor asked.

"I am changing my wheels like daddy does on the car," answered Johnny.

Most little boys seek to be like their fathers. Most little girls seek to play house just like mother. We as children of a Heavenly Father should seek to work as he works. The most miserable person in the world is one who has nothing to do, nothing to demand his time and effort — or who simply does not care to work.

We were created in the image of one who worked. We should strive to live up to that image.

> If God measured everybody else by me,
> How near the mark do you s'pose they'd be?
> Would they leave steps as they pass this way,
> Through sands of Time, that men might say,
> "We found the church in their lives revealed"?
> His word of Life in their hearts concealed."
> Oh, a beacon light I'd strive to be
> If God measured everybody else by me.
> — W. D. Smith

*Prayer*: Lead us through the hours of the day that we may walk as we would have our children walk. In the name of one who set a perfect example we pray. Amen.

## The Blessed Yoke

*"It is good for a man that he bear the yoke in his youth."*
— Lamentations 3:27

*"Take my yoke upon you, and learn of me; for I am meek and lowly in heart; and ye shall find rest unto your souls. For my yoke is easy, and my burden is light."* — Matthew 11:29, 30

Susan owned a small parakeet. Often she hung his cage on the screened back porch and opened the door. The little bird would fly all around and have a wonderful time. If strangers came in and began to talk, the bird would quickly fly to the cage and go inside. Susan would say, "He feels safer in his cage."

There are many kinds of bondage that make people happy. A father is happy to go home at night to his wife and children. They are the reason he is bound to his job and must work hard. Yet he is happy.

Children who are taught to obey their parents are happier than children who have no demands made upon them. They know what to depend upon and feel secure.

Christians who take the yoke of Christ find their life restricted in some ways but they are happy. Like children they know who will take care of them, and on whom they can depend.

> Then hold my hand, most gracious God,
> Guide all my goings still;
> And let it be my life's one aim,
> To know and do thy will.

*Prayer*: We thank thee for thy care and providence for us. Give us grace to live and serve thee as we should. In the name of Jesus our Lord we pray. Amen.

## Tragic Treasures

*"But God said unto him, Thou fool, this night thy soul shall be required of thee: then whose shall those things be, which thou hast provided?"*

*"So is he that layeth up treasures for himself, and is not rich toward God."* — Luke 12:20, 21

We see the truth of the above text illustrated in our country today. America is a rich nation. More people have comfortable homes and plenty of food and luxuries than ever before. Yet our people are unhappy, restless and dissatisfied. As a result our nation is filled with crime. People are afraid to walk on the streets alone at night. Even in the daytime some heinous crimes are committed. What has gone wrong? We have forgotten God and turned to self-indulgence. Those who seek to lay up treasures for themselves are losing their souls. How tragic!

> Here lies a miser
> Who lived for himself,
> Winter and Summer, gathering pelf;
> Now where he is and how he fares,
> Nobody knows and nobody cares.
> — Found on a tombstone

*Prayer*: Help us, O God, to put away any sin or possession that would keep us from serving thee. For Christ's sake we pray. Amen.

98

## Every Candle Counts

*"Ye are the light of the world. A city that is set on an hill cannot be hid. Neither do men light a candle and put it under a bushel, but on a candlestick; and it giveth light unto all that are in the house."* — Matthew 5:14, 15

We read in the papers that the great evangelist, Billy Graham, was coming to our town for a one-night service. Most of us had never had an opportunity to see or hear him. People went to the service in great numbers. I do not remember the sermon and I do not remember the songs, but I remember the lights. As we went through the turnstile at the door each person was handed a small candle and a match. At a certain time in the service all were asked to light their candles and hold them up. All other lights were off for the moment. What an impressive sight!

Often when I am tempted to think that my life is of no consequence or worth I remember all the thousands of candles shining that night and how all together they made a beautiful sight.

God has given each person on earth some kind of light to shine, and some purpose for shining that light.

Trim your feeble lamp, my brother: ·
Some poor sailor tempest tossed,
Trying now to make the harbor,
In the darkness may be lost.

Let the lower lights be burning!
Send a gleam across the wave!
Some poor fainting, struggling sea-man,
You may rescue, you may save.

*Prayer*: May the light of Christ's love shine from our lives today. We pray in the name of Jesus our Lord. Amen.

## Take Heed Lest You Fall

*"Wherefore let him that thinketh he standeth take heed lest he fall."* — I Corinthians 10:12

We are all blind until we see
That in the human plan
Nothing is worth the making if
It does not make the man.

Why build these cities glorious
If man unbuilded goes?

In vain we build the work, unless
The builder also grows.
— Edwin Markham

We are often tempted to think we are more important or better equipped than the other fellow. Then we make ourselves weak, and fail where we should have succeeded.

Look at Peter in the Bible. He was so proud of himself. He felt he would follow Jesus in spite of all hardship! Yet, when the test came he denied knowing Christ. True, he was broken-hearted afterward, but then it was too late to recall his denial.

Another giant character in the Bible was Samson. He was very strong physically but he gave his strength away carelessly — and suffered the consequences.

When we think we can whip the world alone, we need to take stock and see if we are depending too much on self. The old proverb still holds, "Pride goeth before destruction, and a haughty spirit before a fall."

*Prayer*: Dwell in our hearts as thou didst dwell with the mighty men of old. We ask in the name of Jesus our Saviour. Amen.

## Who Are You?

*"My soul cleaveth unto the dust: quicken thou me according to thy word."* — Psalm 119:25

Within my earthly temple there's a crowd:
There's one of us that's humble, one that's proud,
There's one that's broken-hearted for his sins,
And one that unrepentant sits and grins,
There's one that cares for nought but fame and self.
From much perplexing care I would be free
If I could once determine which is Me!

As children we used to play a game called "Who Am I?" We would pretend to be someone and the other children would try to guess who we were by asking us questions.

Sometimes we need to stop and ask ourselves the question, "Who am I?"

Are we the person our family sees each day at home — or are we the person our friends meet at social gatherings? Are we the same person wherever we may be?

The books we read, the magazines we look at, the places we go all have a part in making us the person we are. If we want to be a kind person we will think about kind things. If we want to be a good student we will spend time studying. If we want to be looked upon with respect we will make sure we choose people with high ideals for our companions.

Who are you? Who do you want to be? Seek to develop into that person.

*Prayer*: Father, we may at times grow discouraged and wonder who we are. Help us always to remember we are children of the King of kings. We thank thee for thy love towards us. For Jesus' sake we pray. Amen.

## Christ's Trustworthy Directions

*"In all thy ways acknowledge him, and he shall direct thy paths."* — Proverbs 3:6

*". . . but wisdom is profitable to direction."*

— Ecclesiastes 10:10

We were about to make a turn at a dangerous intersection. The car coming toward us was signaling that he would be turning. This meant that the way would be clear for us. Just as my husband started to accelerate the car and make the turn he followed an urge to wait, and said, "Sometimes people drive along with the turn signal on when they have no plan for turning."

Sure enough, in a flash the car with turn signal still flashing whizzed by, going straight ahead. If we had accepted his signal and turned, a horrible wreck would have resulted.

Christ's directions are sure and safe. We can follow them in perfect assurance. Many young people, and older, follow the signals of false leaders and their lives are hopelessly wasted, if not horribly wrecked.

To every man there openeth
A way, and ways, and a way,
And the high soul climbs the high way,
And the low soul gropes the low:
And in between, on the misty flats,
The rest drift to and fro.
But to every man there openeth
A high way and a low,
And every man decideth
The way his soul shall go.

— John Oxenham

*Prayer*: Help us remember today that no one else can do the work thou hast assigned to us. May we place our lives in thy hands and be directed of thee. In Jesus' name we pray. Amen.

## Give Your Best to Receive Your Best

*"Cast thy bread upon the waters: for thou shalt find it after many days."* — Ecclesiastes 11:1

Two little girls were sitting side by side on the doorstep. They were hugging each other and showing their mutual affection. Soon they were up running and playing. Little Lynn accidently hit Janie with a ball. Suddenly Janie said ugly things to Lynn and the child ran home crying.

When they gave love to each other they were happy. When they became angry and gave ugly words they received ugly words in return. So it is throughout life.

> Give to the world the best that you have,
> And its best will come back to you.
> Give love and love to your heart will flow,
> And strength to your inmost needs.
> Have faith and scores of hearts will show
> Their faith in your work and deeds.
> For life is a mirror for king and for slave
> 'Tis just what we are and do.
> So give the world the best that you have
> And its best will come back to you.

*Prayer:* Dear Lord, help me to give my best each day to all I chance to meet. May I serve and be a blessing without thought of what it will cost or what it will return. Amen.

## Responsible for God's Packages

*"And the Lord said unto Cain, Where is Abel thy brother? And he said, I know not: Am I my brother's keeper?"*
— Genesis 4:9

Leaving my car at the entrance to a downtown parking lot I saw a large sign. It read, "We are not responsible for packages left in cars."

The thought came to me, "But I am responsible for the package of life God has given me." So I walked a bit more carefully across the busy intersection. But that did not satisfy me for I remembered the words of Cain, "Am I my brother's keeper?"

It is not enough to be careful for ourselves; we have others to think about, too. If we are Christians we are responsible to God for our brothers.

One of the blind poet's songs reminds us of our duty.

Rescue the perishing, Care for the dying,
Snatch them in pity from sin and the grave;
Weep o'er the erring one, Lift up the fallen,
Tell them of Jesus the mighty to save.

Rescue the perishing, Care for the dying;
Jesus is merciful, Jesus will save.

— Fanny J. Crosby

*Prayer*: Help us Heavenly Father to realize we are our brother's keeper. Amen.


## Showing Sympathy

*"Bear ye one another's burdens, and so fulfil the law of Christ."*
— Galatians 6:2

The big business man slipped onto a stool and ordered a cup of coffee. The cafe was a small one in a New Mexico village. The owner-operator-cook-waiter was lonely.

"Where are you from?" he asked his customer.

"Lubbock, Texas," was the reply.

"Oh, I knew a man from Lubbock. He owned a ranch near here." The proprietor was all smiles. He mentioned the rancher's name, and asked, "Ever heard of him?"

The business man thought of a beautiful home near his own. He thought of the rancher's widow living there alone. "He and his wife were some of our closest friends. We miss him since he died."

As men in a lonely place will do, they talked about their mutual friend. The one had known him in a social way, the other as a big rancher in a small town.

"Well, I'll tell you one thing. We all thought well of him in this community. He was quick to go where sympathy was needed, and willing to stay and help with the work."

To show sympathy is a most wonderful trait,
And it's one that is too hard to find;
But a better trait still is to never be late
With help that is tender and kind.

— J. T. Bolding

*Prayer*: Lord, help us to be thoughtful of the needs of others; always ready to be helpful in time of need. In Jesus' name we pray Amen.

## Expecting the Best

*"But, beloved, we are persuaded better things of you, and things that accompany salvation, though we thus speak."*

— Hebrews 6:9

Jack was a rowdy in school. All the teachers dreaded him.

One fall a new teacher came to the school. He began to keep Jack so busy doing things the boy simply forgot to be rowdy. One day Jack fell back into his old ways, and knocked one of the other pupils down. The teacher took the fallen boy and comforted him. To Jack he merely said, "Jack, I expect better things from you."

Jack became a great success in life because that teacher in a quiet way brought out the very best by believing it was there — and expecting it.

There are loyal hearts, there are spirits brave,
There are souls that are pure and true;
Then give the world the best you have,
And the best will come back to you.

Give the truth, and you will be paid in kind,
And a song with a song will meet;
The smile which is sweet will surely find
Other smiles that are just as sweet.

For life is a mirror of king and slave —
'Tis just what we are, and do:
Then give to the world the best that you have,
And the best will come back to you.

— Madeline S. Bridges

*Prayer*: Dear Heavenly Father, help us today to be our best. May we be kind to the lonely, and helpful to those in need. Give us the desire to be our best in work and in play. Amen.

## In Times of Loneliness

*". . . and, lo, I am with you alway, even unto the end of the world."* — Matthew 28:20

*"Thou shalt increase my greatness, and comfort me on every side."* — Psalm 71:21

Did you ever walk around in the midst of thousands of people and feel lonely? That was just how I felt at a convention which I was attending in our town. Then I saw an old friend across the hall and we were soon engaged in conversation.

Life is lonely at times for the person who is a Christian. He often feels that all the world is passing him by. But he need not feel lonely. Jesus has promised always to be with us. He is at our side day and night. When we feel lonely we should just talk to God. He is there close by, ready to hear. And this is interesting. When we have finished talking to God he will often lead us to someone who also needs a friend or to someone to whom we can witness.

One is walking with me over life's uneven way,
Constantly supporting me each moment of the day;
How can I be lonely when such fellowship is mine,
　　With my blessed Lord divine!

In life's rosy morning when the skies above are clear,
In its noontide hours with many cares and problems near,
Or when evening shadows fall at closing of my day
　　Jesus will be there alway.

— Haldor Lillenas

*Prayer*: Our heavenly Father, help us today to remember thou wilt never fail nor forget thy children. If trouble should come, help us to know thou art there to comfort and care. We thank thee for thy presence always. Amen.

## A Letter from God

*"The Lord make his face shine upon thee, and be gracious unto thee: The Lord lift up his countenance upon thee, and give thee peace."* — Numbers 6:25, 26

Each day Marilyn ran to meet the postman. There would be letters for Mother or Daddy, but none for her.

"Why don't you bring me a letter?" she asked the postman.

"I see a letter God has written you," the postman replied. "Look at the little green leaves coming up in the flower bed. God is telling you Spring is here."

All day the little girl was happy. God had written her a letter. She saw God in the trees, in the animals running down the walk, and in the refreshing shower of rain that fell in the afternoon.

God writes every person in the world a love letter if he only has eyes to see it and read it. If we see God in the beautiful earth he has created his face will shine upon us and give us peace.

Alas for him who never sees
The stars shine through his cypress-trees!

Who, hopeless, lays his dead away,
Nor looks to see the breaking day. . . .

— Whittier

*Prayer*: Father, help us to see today the beauties in nature. Help us to realize thou hast made the earth for us to enjoy and care for. Give us the realization that as a seed dies it is born again to come forth in new beauty. Amen.

## The Waves and Tides of Life

*"The steps of a good man are ordered by the Lord: and he delighteth in his way. Though he fall, he shall not be utterly cast down: for the Lord upholdeth him with his hand."*

— Psalm 37:23, 24

One summer we visited the seashore with our two small grandsons. The boys had so much fun standing on the beach and letting the waves wash over their feet and legs. They laughed and jumped as children do. Then they found an empty can. They would throw the can as far out in the water as possible, and then it would come riding back on a wave. They were really having fun.

Suddenly a larger than usual wave came in and the boys were tossed to the ground and were covered with water. They struggled to their feet and were about to cry when their mother called out, "That was a big one, but you managed fine." They laughed again and went on having fun.

Suddenly they noticed their can had drifted far away and would not come back. They were disappointed, but soon found something else to interest them and went on having a good time.

Life is like that. Sometimes we are cast down by the tides of life. Sometimes we lose something very precious and dear — but always we must go on. And God speaks words of encouragement. God will give us the strength and courage to face it all.

In shady green pastures, so rich and so sweet,
God leads his dear children along;
Where the water's cold flow bathes the weary one's feet,
God leads his dear children along.

*Prayer*: Dear Father, help us to trust in thy leadership and care, in the valleys as well as on the mountain top. Amen.

## What to Carry When You're Climbing Life's Mountains

*"Thou shalt worship the Lord thy God, and him only shalt thou serve."* — Matthew 4:10

We start at the bottom on our climb through life. We start as new-born babies and slowly climb to adulthood. And throughout our journey of life there are hills to climb. Sometimes the climb is difficult. But there are things we can take along that will make it easier and happier.

First of all we must carry love for God in our hearts. You will be surprised how much this will help to make the climb easier. Then we must take with us love for our fellow man. We must take along consideration for others. Others also are climbing life's highest hill and they might need a helping hand.

> Many are calling for light from on high,
> Then let us help while we may;
> Will we not answer their pitiful cry?
> Oh, help somebody to-day.
>
> Out on the mountain of folly and sin
> Far from the straight narrow way;
> Who then will help bring the wanderer in?
> Oh, help somebody to-day.
>
> From early morning till cometh the night,
> Patiently labor and pray;
> Turning the lost from the wrong to the right,
> Oh, help somebody to-day.
>
> — W. J. Henry

*Prayer*: Our Father, help us today to realize the way up is down to service. May we realize true greatness comes from being right in our hearts and may we be like Jesus in heart and action and spirit. Amen.

## The Ladder Is Still There

*"Blessed is the man that endureth temptation: for when he is tried, he shall receive the crown of life, which the Lord hath promised to them that love him."* — James 1:12

Many years ago on Lincoln's birthday a cartoon appeared in some of the newspapers. The cartoon pictured a log cabin close to the base of a high mountain. On top of the mountain was pictured the White House. Against the side of the mountain was pictured a ladder. The foot of the ladder touched the cabin, and the top rung reached the mansion on the top of the mountain. The caption read, "The ladder is still there."

Young people need to realize there is a ladder to climb. They may not all reach the top but God promises a reward for those who try to succeed in life. There are still men today who have had to climb a long ladder to success.

> Courage, brother, do not stumble,
>     Though thy path be dark as night;
> There's a star to guide the humble;
>     Trust in God and do the right.

*Prayer*: Our Father, we thank thee, that thy mercies are still upon us. We thank thee for the love thou dost shed around us. Let thy everlasting arms be underneath us as we seek to climb higher each day. Help us to seek and do thy will always. We ask in the name of Jesus Christ. Amen.

## Understanding Neighbors

*"Love worketh no ill to his neighbor."* — Romans 13:10

We were so surprised one afternoon soon after we moved into a new home to have a large group of neighbors drop in. They brought cold drinks and cookies and made a party out of the visit. Isn't it wonderful to have friends and congenial neighbors!

But ill-tempered or suspicious neighbors can be a source of much unhappiness. One of my friends is constantly having a feud with some of her neighbors. If they happen to let the lawn sprinkler get near her car as it stands in the drive she tries to make them pay for having the car washed. She does not enjoy her neighbors. She is always unhappy.

> If we knew the cares and crosses
> Crowding 'round our neighbor's way
> If we knew of all his losses
> Sorely grievous day by day;
> Would we then so often chide him
> Casting o'er his life a shadow,
> Leaning on his heart a strain?
>
> Let us reach into our bosoms
> For the key to other lives,
> And with love to erring nature,
> Cherish good that still survives;

So that when our disrobed spirits
Soar to realms of light again,
We may say, dear Father, judge us
As we judged our fellow men.

*Prayer*: Holy Father, as we come into thy presence help us to examine our hearts and purge out any evil thoughts toward our neighbors. We ask for the sake of Christ. Amen.

## The Shaper of Our Lives

*"And the vessel that we made of clay was marred in the hands of the potter; so he made it again another vessel. . . ."*
— Jeremiah 18:4

*"We are the clay, and thou our potter; and we all are the work of thy hand."* — Isaiah 64:8

Once as we traveled through the state of Alabama we stopped at a charming cottage where clay pots were for sale. The owner was also the potter. For our benefit and interest he put some clay on his potter's wheel and shaped a graceful vase while we watched, fascinated. Around the small shop he had all shapes and sizes of clay products to sell, all made by his hands.

How interesting it is to think of God as the great potter who shapes all kinds of lives and directs them.

When the potter places a piece of clay on the wheel he has in mind exactly what he wants to mold. God has a plan for everyone of us, and only if we submit our lives into his hands will we find happiness and success. We always should be careful to seek to know God's will for our lives. His plan is best.

Thy will, O God, not mine, be done!
I know thy will is best;
If, sometimes, otherwise it seems,
I still believe and rest.

Thy will is best, — 'tis there I rest;
In shadow or in sun,
My prayer to thee shall ever be:
Thy perfect will be done.
— T. O. Chisholm

*Prayer*: Dear Heavenly Father, make known to us what thou wouldst have us be. Let all be glorious within our hearts as we submit to thy will. In the name of Christ we pray. Amen.

## A Woman's Rights

*"He maketh the barren woman to keep house, and to be a joyful mother of children. Praise ye the Lord." —* Psalm 113:9

The rights of women — what are they?
The right to labor and to pray,
The right to watch while others sleep,
The right o'er others' woes to weep,
The right to succor in distress,
The right while others curse to bless,
The right to love while others scorn,
The right to comfort all who mourn,
The right to shed new joy on earth,
The right to feel the soul's high worth,
The right to lead the soul to God
Along the path the Saviour trod.

I know a young mother who was left alone with two small children to rear. She was forced to get a job and work to keep food and clothing for them. Each Sunday found her sitting with them in the sanctuary. She gave to them every spare moment she could take away from her work. Often I thought how fortunate they were to have a mother who loved them so much. Of this world's goods they had barely enough — but of love they had an abundance.

Fortunate indeed is the child who has a good mother.

*Prayer*: O God, our Holy Father, we thank thee today for giving us gentle mothers, patient mothers, long-suffering and kind mothers. Help us always to appreciate our mothers and their self-sacrifice shown for us. For the sake of Christ we pray. Amen.

## Obeying God Rather Than Pleasing Men

*"We must obey God rather than men." —* Acts 5:29

Tom was a very young business man, and he was anxious to succeed. He was happy with his work and the future looked bright to him. One day a very prominent man asked him to go to lunch with him. The man tried to find out all he could about Tom's boss. Tom did not say much. Finally the man came to the point and said: "I will make it worth your while if you will get a certain list of names from your boss' files for me."

Tom wanted the man's favor very much, and he knew just where the list was kept. "I will think about it," said Tom.

That night Tom kept repeating the verse, "Thou shalt not steal."

Next morning his wife asked him what had kept him awake so much. "I am facing a decision," said Tim. "I can get a list of names of our customers for another business and make a nice sum of money."

"Why Tom, you should never give such a thing a second thought," exclaimed his wife. "Isn't it better to obey God than please men?"

Tom called the man and refused to do as he wished.

*Prayer*: Dear Father, fill our hearts with the love that prompts courage in the face of temptation. Help us always to take a stand for the right. For Christ's sake we pray. Amen.

## Exercising Our Talents

*"Now in the morning as he returned to the city, he hungered. And when he saw a fig tree in the way, he came to it, and found nothing thereon. . . ."* — Matthew 21:18-22

Does Christ come to your life seeking fruit and find none? You have some talent; use it to the best of your ability and you will gain more talent. Refuse to use what talent you have and you will soon lose it completely.

Two sisters were gifted singers. One readily and cheerfully agreed to always sing when asked. The other always waited to be begged. As time went on the first sister was increasingly in demand. The other was seldom and finally never asked.

God comes to us with opportunities and as we respond willingly he uses us more and more. If we fail time and time again to respond we are soon left out.

The fig tree was cursed for bearing no fruit.

> A sacred burden in this life ye bear,
> Look on it, bear it solemnly,
> Stand up and walk beneath it steadfastly;
> Fail not for sorrow, falter not for sin,
> But onward, upward, till the goal ye win.
> — Frances Anne Kemble

*Prayer*: Our Gracious Heavenly Father, the bountiful giver of all good and precious gifts, we thank thee. We thank thee for the talents we have. Help us to use our gifts to bear fruit for thy kingdom. May we dedicate our lives for service to thee each day. Teach us how to bear the most fruit. In the name of Jesus Christ our Saviour we pray. Amen.

## Spiritual Housecleaning

*"Wherefore seeing we also are compassed about with so great a cloud of witnesses, let us lay aside every weight, and the sin which doth so easily beset us, and let us run with patience the race that is set before us."* — Hebrews 12:1

Some women are just naturally better housekeepers than others. Most of us get by on our housecleaning but what about cleansing our minds!

I read of a convict who resented the world. Each time he was released from prison he tried to get revenge and got into new trouble. At last a kind man won his confidence and showed him he must clean up his own heart and thoughts. The man put aside the thought of getting revenge and spent his time trying to help other ex-convicts find a place in life. In this way he found true usefulness and happiness.

> I have Jesus dwelling with me
> Every hour of every day,
> So whatever may befall me,
> "All is well," my heart can say.
>
> In this world of living pleasure
> "Jesus only" would I know;
> Satisfied His steps to follow,
> And His great salvation know.
>
> — Mrs. C. H. Morris

*Prayer:* Almighty Father, help us today to cast out of our lives the things which would keep us from serving thee. Help us to remember we are precious in thy sight and seek to serve thee better. In the name of our Lord Jesus we pray. Amen.

## Shoes of a Lifetime, Shoes of Love

*"For unto everyone that hath shall be given, and he shall have abundance: but from him that hath not shall be taken away even that which he hath."* — Matthew 25:29

For more than thirty years a man in Boston saved his children's outgrown shoes. Finally three hundred pairs of shoes hung in the attic. They told the story from birth to adulthood of four children. A reporter heard about the shoes and wrote a story. A doctor working for a school for retarded children read the story. He called and asked for the shoes to be used in his school. They were gladly given. That man's thrift helped others who could not help themselves.

We must make what we have count for good. There are many ways to find uses for our material goods as well as our talents.

> Somebody did a golden deed,
>     Proving himself a friend in need;
> Somebody sang a cheerful song,
>     Brightening the sky the whole day long,
>
> Somebody made a loving gift,
>     Cheerfully tried a load to lift;
> Somebody told the love of Christ,
>     Told how His will was sacrificed,
>
> Was that somebody you?
>
> — John R. Clements

*Prayer*: Dear Father, we thank thee for giving us talents with which to serve thee. Help us to have the attitude of willingness to help others. For the sake of Christ Jesus we pray. Amen.

## Playing for Pride

*"Hosanna to the son of David: Blessed is he that cometh in the name of the Lord: Hosanna in the highest."*

> — Matthew 21:9

The Scripture above gives us a picture of Jesus when he was being honored and praised. He never once acted proud or haughty. Through all honor or mistreatment he remained meek and lowly.

A boy on the high school football team was always glad when he could make a touchdown. Whenever he could get his hands on the ball he raced for the goal. He liked to hear the fans call his name and praise him! One day the coach suspended him from the team for two weeks. He was shocked.

"I am your best player. Why mistreat me?" he exclaimed.

"Praise has gone to your head," replied the coach. "As a result, you refuse to work with the rest of the team so that you may have all the praise for yourself."

> Is anybody happier
>     Because you passed his way?
> Does anyone remember
>     That you spoke to him today?

This day is almost over,
    And its toiling time is through;
Is there anyone to utter now,
    A friendly word for you?

Did you waste the day, or lose it?
    Was it well or poorly spent?
Did you leave a trail of kindness,
    Or a scar of discontent?

*Prayer*: Our Father, help us when we have been triumphant and successful to remain humble. May we ever give thee the praise and glory for the blessings which come our way. May we never be proud and haughty. For the sake of Jesus Christ our Lord we pray. Amen.

## Clothing Ourselves with Kindness

*"And be ye kind one to another, tenderhearted, forgiving one another, even as God for Christ's sake hath forgiven you."*

— Ephesians 4:32

There is a destiny that makes us brothers;
    None goes his way alone:
All that we send into the lives of others
    Comes back into our own.

— Edwin Markham

It would take pages and pages to tell all the ways we can be kind to one another. If we look up and see the millions of stars at night we marvel at their number and beauty. Ways of showing kindness are just as numerous and just as beautiful. Our lives can become beautiful if we clothe ourselves with kindness.

Let's resolve to begin or increase our deeds of kindness at once. We can show kindness by forgiving others, and by concern for the feelings of others.

We should be kind to all. Why should we be kind even to those who mistreat us? Because God sent his son to die for us and has forgiven us our sins.

*Prayer*: Father, as we come before thee may we determine to develop a better attitude in our relationship with others. Help us to be forgiving of those who offend us. Control our tongues as we speak to others. For the sake of one who was never unkind, Jesus Christ, we pray. Amen.

## Go Inside and Sit Down

*"Blessed are they that dwell in thy house: they will be still praising thee."* — Psalm 84:4

One morning I went to a sidewalk sale. People were milling about examining the merchandise. Two ladies were in front of a table filled with boots. They were attempting to try on the boots standing up. After they had almost fallen several times they found some they thought were suitable and took them to the check out desk.

"You could go inside the store and sit down to try them on," the clerk said.

"We have already decided on these," replied the ladies. And they paid their money and went away.

How often we make things harder by not inquiring which way is best. We stumble and fall and get misfits because it takes more time to go into the house of the Lord and ask his directions for our decisions.

*Prayer:* Grant to us, most loving Father, the ability to find what is thy purpose for our lives. May we find comfort and guidance in thy house. In the name of Christ our Lord we pray. Amen.

## Bearing Burdens

*"Bear ye one another's burdens, and so fulfil the law of Christ."*
— Galatians 6:2

Mack and Joe were brothers. Each day they walked to school together. Always Mack carried Joe's books. One day a lady was sitting on her porch and she called to the boys, "Why doesn't the little boy carry the books sometimes?"

"Because I like to carry them," Mack replied. Had the woman looked closer, she would have noticed that because Joe had deformed hands and arms he could only carry something very light.

When Joe and Mack were adults there came a time in Mack's life when he needed to borrow some money. Joe had become a successful business man. He was glad to let Mack have the money. Said Joe, "This is to help pay you for all the times when you carried my books and helped me get back and forth to school."

I need the lives of others
  To make my life complete;
I need your recognition
  To light my humble street.

Some friends are rich, some are poor,
And some have moderate fee —
I treasure every one of them,
They mean so much to me.

— Walter Werner

*Prayer*: Father, help us to be worthy of those friends who help us bear our burdens each day. In the name of Christ we pray. Amen.

## " . . . Not to Be Ministered to . . . "

*"And whosoever will be great among you, let him be your servant: Even as the Son of man came not to be ministered unto, but to minister, and to give his life a ransom for many."*

— Matthew 20:27, 28

Leta was a small girl but she liked to help her mother with the housework. Often she waited to run and play until the work was finished. One summer the neighbors invited her to go on a vacation trip with them.

"Why did you ask Leta and not me?" her brother asked.

"We have noticed how much Leta works around the house and we thought she deserved a trip," the neighbor replied.

Jesus lived a life of service. He would have enjoyed just staying in his wonderful home in heaven, but because we needed salvation he came to earth to make a way for us to share that home.

No service in itself is small,
None great, though earth it fill;
But that is small that seeks its own
And great that seeks God's will.
Then hold my hand, most gracious God,
Guide all my goings still;
And let it be my life's one aim
To know and do thy will.

*Prayer*: We thank thee, our Father, for places to serve in this great world. Help us to share our faith with others and keep our doubts to ourselves. We thank thee for those who have unselfishly served to spread thy kingdom. Accept our prayer for Jesus' sake. Amen.

## Searching for a Home

*"We look for new heavens and a new earth wherein dwelleth righteousness."* — II Peter 3:13

Have you ever been seeking a lost key or some other important item? You became so fascinated with the search that all else was forgotten until you were successful in finding what you looked for. We look for a home in heaven and we should be so fascinated with our preparation and search for that home that all else takes second place.

We must invite others to search with us also. There will never be too many seeking that heavenly home.

As you try to ascend the steep mountains of life
    Which seem always to stand in your way,
And you try to supply someone's need in the strife,
    You'll find out you need help every day.
For your needs, on your climb, to the Saviour then look.
    Says his word, his supply is complete.
With his presence assured, as he says in his book,
    Every day in his way is so sweet!

— J. T. Bolding

*Prayer*: O God, indwell in our hearts today. Give us love and patience to face the problems of the day. May we recognize the saving power of hope in Christ our Lord. May we feel the wonderful fascination of life as we prepare and look for our eternal home. In the name of one who died for our sins we pray. Amen.

## Brotherly Love

*"He that loveth his brother abideth in the light, and there is none occasion of stumbling in him. But he that hateth his brother is in darkness, and walketh in darkness, and knoweth not whither he goeth, because that darkness hath blinded his eyes."*
— I John 2:10, 11

I have a friend who is a very successful lawyer. I often wondered why his brothers were just plain business men and seemed not to have gone to school past high school. When their mother died I attended the funeral. The minister told how the father had died when the children were small, leaving the mother without funds. The older boys had left school and worked to support the family. They had sacrificed to send their younger brother and sister to college. The lawyer had told the minister of his brothers' unselfishness and wanted them recognized that day.

Give us, Lord, a chance to be
Our goodly best, brave, wise and free,
Our goodly best for ourself, and others,
Till all men learn to live as brothers."

— English Prayer

*Prayer*: Dear Lord, help us to love our brothers as we love ourselves. Help us to follow the teaching of Jesus Christ, thy son. Pardon us when we are selfish and forget others. May we learn to be merciful to all men and treat them as brothers. We ask in the name of Jesus Christ. Amen.

## Storehouses of Treasure

*"We have thought of thy lovingkindness, O God, in the midst of thy temple."* — Psalm 48:9

"To get peace, if you do want it, make for yourselves nests of pleasant thoughts. None of us yet knows, for none of us has been taught in early youth, what fairy palaces we may build of beautiful thoughts — proof against all adversity. Bright fancies, satisfied memories, noble histories, faithful sayings, treasure-houses of precious and restful thoughts, which cannot disturb, nor pain, make gloomy, nor poverty take away from us — houses built without hands for our souls to live in." — Ruskin.

Let us, then, labor for an inward stillness —
An inward stillness and an inward healing;
That perfect silence where the lips and heart
Are still, and we no longer entertain
Our own imperfect thoughts and vain opinions,
But God alone speaks in us, and we wait
In singleness of heart, that we may know
His will, and in the silence of our spirits,
That we may do His will, and do that only.

— Longfellow

*Prayer*: Our Father in heaven, help us today to develop kind thoughts. Give us quiet and meditation that we may correct our mistaken thoughts and formulate wise plans. Give us inward silence and stillness as we wait to know the will of our God. We pray in the name of Jesus, thy son. Amen.

## Laying Up Treasures in Heaven

*"Lay not up for yourselves treasures upon earth, where moth and rust doth corrupt, and where thieves break through and steal: But lay up for yourselves treasures in heaven, where neither moth nor rust down corrupt, and where thieves do not break through nor steal: For where your treasure is, there will your heart be also."* — Matthew 6:19-21

Our Lord teaches that spiritual treasure is permanently superior to material treasure. We cannot serve two masters. We must choose where our main treasure will be stored. How can we lay up treasures in heaven?

We can share our material wealth to help carry on the work of the church. We can give the personal touch of help to those in need. God looks at how much we keep for ourselves as well as what we give.

> Let me go where saints are going,
>   To the mansions of the blest;
> Let me go where my Redeemer
>   Has prepared His people's rest.
> I would gain the realms of brightness,
>   Where they dwell for evermore;
> I would join the friends that wait me,
>   Over on the other shore.
>   Let me go; 'tis Jesus calls me;
>     Let me gain the realms of day;
>   Bear me over, angel pinions;
>     Longs my soul to be away.
>
> — L. Hartsough

*Prayer*: Our Father, make us grateful for thy blessings as we lay up our treasure in heaven. For Jesus sake we pray. Amen.

## Still in Need of the Story

*"Go ye therefore, and teach all nations, baptizing them in the name of the Father, and of the Son, and of the Holy Ghost."*

— Matthew 28:19

The world grows smaller each year. With jet airliners we can travel farther in a day than most of our parents traveled in a lifetime. Yet Christ's great commission is still in effect today. We are still obligated to go and tell the story.

If ever Jesus has need of me,
  Somewhere in the fields of sin,
I'll go where the darkest places be,
  And let the sunshine in;
I'll be content with the lowliest place,
  To earth's remotest rim,
I know I'll see his smiling face,
  If it's done with a thought of Him.

The lowliest deed will be reckoned great
  In the book that the angels keep,
If it helps another along the road
  That is often rough and steep.

A kindly word may let sunshine in,
  Where life's rays are sadly dim;
And love can win a soul for God
  If it's done with a thought of Him.

— Chas. H. Gabriel

*Prayer*: Dear Father, give us more zeal to labor in thy vineyard. Give us more strength in daily prayer to go out seeking the lost in this world. May we make an earnest effort today to witness for thee. For we ask in the name of our Lord and Saviour Jesus Christ. Amen.

## If We Could Laugh Instead of Worry!

*"A merry heart maketh a cheerful countenance: but by sorrow of the heart the spirit is broken."* — Proverbs 15:13

People are born with an instinct for happiness. We wish to be happy. How can we be happy and have a merry heart?

James was walking to school. He felt just plain mad. Breakfast had not been to his liking. Sister Jane had hurried off to walk with her chum. James trudged along cross and angry. Just then Mrs. Royace came out of her door.

"James, would you walk along with me and hold my dog's leash?" she called.

James took the leash. He liked Mrs. Royace's dog.

"Why don't you sit on the porch while I take your dog for a walk?" asked James. And he hurried off with the dog. After a few moments James came back, happy and whistling. He had forgotten his troubles.

If you and I, just you and I
  Should laugh instead of worry;
If we should grow — just you and I
  Kinder and sweeter hearted,
Perhaps in some near by and by
  A good time might get started;
Then what a happy world 'twould be
  For you and me — for you and me.

*Prayer*: Dear Father, help us to find our lost laughter and happiness by helping others. We wish to be excited and happy with life. Give us today the ability to help others and in helping to find true peace and happiness. For the sake of Christ we pray. Amen.

## Life's Diamond

*"And now abideth faith, hope, and love, these three; but the greatest of these is love."* — I Corinthians 13:13

A woman went to a diamond mine to search for diamonds. She found a large stone. After it was polished and cut she had something very valuable.

If the woman had not gone and searched for the diamond she would never have found it. If she had not shared her profits with the owners of the mine she could not have taken the stone away.

Love is like the diamonds in the mine. Love must be searched for. Love must be earned. Love must be polished and kept pure and shining. Love must be shared.

Love thyself last. Look near, behold thy duty
  To those who walk beside thee down life's road;
Make glad their days by little acts of beauty,
  And help them bear the burden of earth's load.

Love thyself last, and thou shalt grow in spirit
  To see, to hear, to know, and understand.
The message of the stars, lo, thou shalt hear it,
  And all God's joys shall be at thy command.

— Ella Wheeler Wilcox

*Prayer*: O God, today help us to go forth to share love and kindness with those about us. Kindle high and holy purposes in our hearts. Teach us to love those about us. We ask in the name of one who loved more than any other, Christ our Saviour. Amen.

## Planting the Right Seed

*"To everything there is a season, and a time to every purpose under the heaven: A time to be born, and a time to die; a time to pluck up that which is planted."* — Ecclesiastes 3:1, 2

This is the time of year when we hate to stay inside. There is so much new life all about us in the great out-of-doors. We have such big plans for what we will plant, and what we will see as our plants grow.

Families are like the springtime. When children are little we plan carefully how we will train and teach them. We want for them the best schools and advantages. We must not forget that what we plant in the child's heart at home will bear fruit throughout his life. We must plant love for others, pluck out ugly habits and ways. God has a purpose for all his children. We must see that they are properly nourished and trained to fulfill that purpose.

> The year's at the spring,
> And day's at the morn;
> Morning's at seven;
> The hillside's dew-pearled;
> The lark's on the wing;
> The snail's on the thorn;
> God's in His heaven, —
> All's right with the world.
>
> — Browning

*Prayer*: Our dear Father, who loved us and planned for us the seasons of life, help us to enjoy to the fullest each one. Help us to find something good and pleasant about each age through which we pass. May we give thee the praise for life. In the name of Christ our Lord we pray. Amen.

## The Fruit of Praise

*"I will praise thee: O Lord my God, with all my heart: and I will glorify thy name for evermore."* — Psalm 86:12

If we would spend our time praising God instead of grumbling we would find joy in our hearts.

When Dick was a teen-ager he had a paper route. When he was older he worked after school in a grocery store. Everybody liked Dick. He was always so polite and cheerful.

One summer Dick was made manager of the produce department in the store. One of the other boys in the store went to the head manager, and asked, "Why did Dick get the job? I have worked here a long time — much longer than he has."

"Because Dick always praises the other workers," said the manager. "He is happy and often whistles as he works. A happy leader gets more work from the other boys."

> Then hide it not, the music of thy soul,
>     Dear sympathy expressed with kindly voice,
> But let it like a shining river roll
>     To deserts dry — to hearts that would rejoice.

> Oh, let the symphony of kindly words
>     Sound for the poor, the friendless, and the weak,
> And He will bless you, He who struck the chords
>     Will strike another when in turn you seek.

*Prayer:* Our Father who art in heaven, may we today praise thy name. May we see the good in those about us and seek to help them on their way. Help us to forget unpleasant things and remember the pearls of character that are good. In the name of Jesus Christ our Lord we pray. Amen.

## Friendships that Last

*"A friend loveth at all times. . . ."* — Proverbs 17:17

Mrs. Lowery and Mrs. Box had been friends since they were girls in school. They visited often, kept each other's children and were just good friends.

Mrs. Lowery's husband was a good business man and so they were soon quite well off. They moved across town to a new home. At first the women called each other and talked on the phone each day. Then they began to see less and less of each other. Then one day Mrs. Lowery heard that her friend's husband had been killed in an accident and her friend was badly hurt. She rushed to the hospital. She took the children to her own home and cared for them many weeks until their mother was released from the hospital.

"You didn't have to go to all that trouble for me," said Mrs. Box.

"You are my friend, and I wanted to help," was Mrs. Lowery's reply.

> There is no friend like an old friend
> Who has shared our morning days,
> No greeting like his welcome,
> No homage like his praise.

Fame is the scentless sunflower,
With gaudy crown of gold;
But friendship is the breathing rose,
With sweets in every fold.

— Oliver Wendell Holmes

*Prayer*: Our Father, make us worthy of our friends. Make us like the friend who gave his life to redeem our souls. For it is in his name we pray. Amen.

## Our Sure Source of Comfort

*"For his anger endureth but a moment; in his favor is life: weeping may endure for a night, but joy cometh in the morning."*

— Psalm 30:5

*"Wherefore comfort one another with these words."*

— I Thessalonians 4:18

Troubles and trials come and go, but our God always remains the same. "He shall gather the lambs with his arms and carry them in his bosom" (Isaiah 40:11).

We are frail and often in need of comfort and strength. God stands ever ready to give us the strength and comfort we need. God's providence never places you where his grace cannot keep you.

Is your heart o'er burdened with its grief and care?
Are you fainting now beneath the cross you bear?
Tell it to Jesus at the place of prayer,
　　Carry all your sorrows to Him.

Do you long for comfort in your sore distress?
Come to Christ your Saviour and your sins confess;
Tell it all to Jesus, He will heal and bless,
　　Carry all your sorrows to Him.

Are you sad and lonely? Is the pathway drear?
Tarry then no longer in your doubt and fear;
Tell it all to Jesus, He is always near,
　　Carry all your sorrows to Him.

*Prayer*: Dear Father, guide us along the way. Help us not to stray from the homeward pathway. Roll away our heavy burdens. Give us the comfort of faith. In the name of our Saviour Jesus Christ we pray. Amen.

## The Salt of the Earth

*"Ye are the salt of the earth: but if the salt have lost his savor, wherewith shall it be salted? it is thenceforth good for nothing, but to be cast out, and trodden under foot."* — Matthew 5:13

One time I became ill and had to go on a diet with very little salt. The food tasted so flat and I found I just didn't want to eat much. We bought salt substitutes but they were not much help. How glad I was when I could again use some salt on my food. Everything seemed so good.

Jesus wants us to be the kind of people who make our community a better place to live. He said that even a few good people can leaven the whole lump. When we are tempted to choose the wrong side of a question for our own gain, we should ask ourselves, "Am I being the salt of the earth?"

> Once I tossed a twig
>     Into a surging spring,
> And watched it quickly ebb
>     Like some unshackled thing.
> Drifting in the current,
>     Independently and free,
> Bobbing with a rhythm,
>     It bounced buoyantly.
>
> Once a word I uttered,
>     And it echoed through the place
> Like a solitary urchin
>     With a tired, and worried face;
> And it struck a note of gladness,
>     And a hope was lifted high;
> It was just an idle gesture,
>     But it turned away a sigh.
>
> — Laurence Estes

*Prayer:* Help us to strive always to be a blessing to those about us. For Jesus sake we pray. Amen.

## Making Every Day Count

*"For man also knoweth not his time: as the fishes that are taken in an evil net, and as the birds that are caught in the snare; so are the sons of men snared in an evil time, when it falleth suddenly upon them."* — Ecclesiastes 9:12

As we approach summer the days keep getting longer. But after June 22, they begin growing shorter again as the year crawls toward autumn and then winter. We should make every day count for good. There is a time in all our lives when we realize that with the passing of each day our life is growing shorter.

Some people fall into the evil net of saying, "It is too late for me to accomplish anything in life." It will be too late only if we let it be. We should keep trying.

I wrote my first book after I was fifty years old. Often I made mistakes typing by the hunt and pound method. Often I would have liked just to lie down and read a good story. Accomplishments are never gained if we get caught in the net of laziness. Today may be the longest day of your life. Seek to use it well.

> Let us then be up and doing,
> With a heart for any fate;
> Still achieving, still pursuing,
> Learn to labor and to wait.
>
> — Longfellow

*Prayer*: Give us this day, dear Father, the courage to do our best, whatever the task may be. Give us a vision of the lost, needy world and a desire to tell them of Christ. For it is in his name we pray. Amen.

### Give Your Soul Time to Catch Up

*"But the path of the just is as the shining light, that shineth more and more unto the perfect day."* — Proverbs 4:18

Very often we hear someone say, "I must stop and catch up." Sometimes they are talking about finances. Sometimes they are talking about physical strength. The housewife is often talking about catching up on her cleaning.

In Africa when the natives have been walking or running a long way, they never say they must stop and rest. They say, "We must stop and give our soul time to catch up."

In this hurried world we desperately need to let our souls have time to catch up. We need to stop and take time to think on beautiful and holy things.

> Stay, stay at home, my heart, and rest;
> Home-keeping hearts are happiest,
> For those that wander they know not where
> Are full of trouble and full of care;
> To stay at home is best.
>
> — Longfellow

*Prayer*: O God, our Almighty Father, help us to calm our restless hearts. Forgive our wrong and foolish quests. Guide us in the way of inward peace. In the name of one who said, "My peace I leave with you," we pray. Amen.

## Why Wear Flimsy Armor?

*"Above all, taking the shield of faith, wherewith ye shall be able to quench all the fiery darts of the wicked. And take the helmet of salvation, and the sword of the Spirit, which is the word of God." —* Ephesians 6:16, 17

Little Jody Alexander loves to play war. He often rushes at his playmates with the lid to the garbage can held in front of him and a long stick for a sword. He feels entirely safe with such fine armor.

How often we go out to meet the world in a warfare with sin with just such flimsy armor! Ephesians 6:11 says: "Put on the whole armor of God, that ye may be able to stand against the wiles of the devil."

A little time in reading
God's word shows me the way
That I should walk and worship
My Lord throughout each day.

A little time in praying
Keeps me within His will,
And brings my heart much gladness
To know He loves me still.

— Jewel Alice McLeod

*Prayer*: Dear Father, we are a land of many faiths and creeds. Help us never to forget that there is only one God — the God who created us, the God who can keep and sustain us in a world of trouble and chaos. Help us to preserve our faith in thee. Help us to show others the way of salvation. In the name of Jesus we pray. Amen.

## Friendship in Action

*"A man that hath friends must show himself friendly; and there is a friend that sticketh closer than a brother."*
— Proverbs 18:24

The Dinwoody family joined the church on Sunday evening. Mr. and Mrs. Lively had never seen them before but they invited them to go home with them for a period of fellowship. That was friendship in action.

A church in the far West where most of the people were far from relatives planned a church-wide Thanksgiving dinner. They became friends in action. We will find life sweeter if we seek ways to show friendship to others.

> This is no time for fear, for doubts of good,
> For broodings on the tragedies of fate.
> It is a time for songs of brotherhood,
> For hymns of joy, of man's divine estate.
> Though echoes of old wars depress the heart,
> Though greed and hate still curse men's nobler ways,
> Though foul suspicion blasts our life apart,
> It is a time for confidence and praise.
> Let prophets prophecy, let poets sing,
> Our dreams are not in vain. The night is past.
> Together, as new hopes are wakening,
> Let us proclaim, The Kingdom Comes at last!
> Our Babels crash. Let selfish flags be furled.
> As brothers all, we build a Friendly World.
>
> — Thomas Curtis Clark

*Prayer*: Dear Father, master of all the universe, help us to show ourselves more friendly to those about us, to those who need to see religion in action. Help us ever to rely on the one friend who sticketh closer than a brother. For in the name of that wonderful friend, Jesus, we pray. Amen.

## Fishers of Men

*"And he saith unto them, Follow me, and I will make you fishers of men."* — Matthew 4:19

A young pastor had eaten lunch with some church members. All they talked about was a fishing trip they had enjoyed lately and another they planned to take in the near future. The young preacher felt a little sorry for himself.

"I am so busy that I have not been able to go fishing in several years," he thought. "Why do I have to work so hard and they have life so easy?"

That night at the church services the minister was dressing for a baptismal service. He wore boots under his robe, to protect his clothes. Suddenly it seemed God spoke to him — "You are a fisher of men. Follow me and I will make your harvest of souls great."

With a light heart he entered the service. From then on when people talked of fishing, he thought and talked of winning the lost.

So I'll win the one next to me,
And you'll win the one next to you;
In all kinds of weather
We'll all work together,
And see what can be done.
So I'll win the one next to me,
And you'll win the one next to you;
In no time at all,
We'll win them all,
Win them, win them, one by one.

*Prayer*: Dear Father, give us power to become fishers of men. Give us courage to seek the lost. In Christ's dear name we pray. Amen.

## "The Vague, Oncoming Years"

*"Whereas ye know not what shall be on the morrow. For what is life? It is even a vapor, that appeareth for a little time, and then vanisheth away."* — James 4:14

The above Scripture tells us how brief life is. I John 2:17 tells us how to live forever, "And the world passeth away, and the lust thereof: but he that doeth the will of God abideth for ever."

In John 3:16 we read, "For God so loved the world that he gave his only begotten son that whosoever believeth on him might not perish but have everlasting life."

In Psalm 16:11 we find that joy in Christ is everlasting, ". . . at thy right hand there are pleasures forevermore."

What though my dreams break on some rock-bound shore
And leave but fragments scattered on the sands!
Shall I be grieving for them evermore,
Or shall I bind them up with eager hands,
And laugh again, and prance again . . . and keep
As souvenirs their broken wings, nor hide
Their scars, nor be afraid Fate yet may sweep
Them back to sea on some outgoing tide?

Why should one fear the vague, oncoming years
If courage speak the final, dauntless word
That puts the seal of silence on our fears?
For I can tell you this: that I have heard
A wondrous melody on Hope's last string,
Seen Winter's icy grip give way to Spring.

*Prayer*: Dear Lord in Heaven, make us ever mindful that thou holdest the keys to life and death. Help us to serve thee in such a way that whether we are on this earth a brief or a long time we will be prepared for the joy eternal, prepared for thy children. In the name of Christ who gave himself for us, we pray. Amen.

## Works that Demonstrate Our Faith

*"For as the body without the spirit is dead, so faith without works is dead also."* — James 2:26

My friend down the street called me on a very cold day: "Could you possibly come and stay with my children for about thirty minutes? I have to run to the school and pick up the older ones."

I was very busy but I loved my friend. And I knew the sudden Norther made it dangerous for little folks to walk far.

The baby was asleep but the four-year-old was very much awake. He brought some of his story books for me to read. We had a lovely time reading, and soon his mother returned.

> He stopped to pat a small dog's head,
> A little thing to do;
> And yet, the dog, remembering,
> Was glad the whole day through.
> He gave a rose into the hand
> Of one who loved it much;
> 'Twas just a rose — but, oh, the joy
> That lay in its soft touch.
>
> He spoke a word so tenderly —
> A word's a wee small thing;
> And yet, it stirred a weary heart
> To hope again, and sing.
>
> — Louis  Snelling

*Prayer*: Our Father, the one to whom we turn in all our trials and problems, we ask thee to make us more aware of the ones around us who are in need of little acts of kindness. For the sake of Christ we pray. Amen.

## The Christian Home

*"And they said one to another, Behold, this dreamer cometh."*
— Genesis 37:19

Joseph is the dreamer mentioned in the first verse. Joseph kept himself pure in order to serve God and he lived in hope that some day his dreams would come true. All young people should keep their hearts and bodies pure so that when the time comes for their dreams to come true, they will be worthy and prepared.

My home must have a high tree
Above its open gate,
My home must have a garden
Where little dreamings wait,
My home must have a wide view
Of field and meadow fair,
Of distant hill, of open sky,
With sunlight everywhere.

My home must have a friendship
With every happy thing,
My home must offer comfort
For any sorrowing,
And every heart that enters
Shall hear its music there,
And find some simple beauty,
That every life may share.
My home must have its mother,
May I grow sweet and wise.
My home must have its father
With honor in his eyes.
My home must have its children;
God grant the parents grace,
To keep our home through all the years,
A kindly, happy place.

*Prayer*: God, give us Christian homes. May we be willing to dedicate them to thee. In the name of Christ. Amen.

## God, Give Us Men!

*"They that seek the Lord shall not want any good thing."*

— Psalm 34:10

Christian fathers want good things for their families. Since goodness comes from God, fathers must first seek God if they are to obtain true goodness for their families.

There is an appointed way to reach the Lord. Jesus said, "I am the way, the truth and the light."

131

When a man seeks to live in God's will, all the blessings he needs will be poured out upon him and his children.

God give us men! A time like this demands
Strong minds, great hearts, true faith, and ready hands;
Men whom the lust of office does not kill;
Men whom the spoils of office cannot buy;
Men who possess opinions and a will;
Men who have honor; men who will not lie;
Men who can stand before a demagogue
And damn his treacherous flatteries without winking;
Tall men, sun-crowned, who live above the fog
In public duty and in private thinking;
For while the rabble with their thumb-worn creeds,
Their large profession and their little deeds,
Mingle in selfish strife, Lo! Freedom weeps,
Wrong rules the land, and waiting justice sleeps.

— J. G. Holland

*Prayer*: Grant the fathers of our day the feel of thy guiding hand upon their lives. May they hear thy voice even amid the tumult of daily work and care. Help the fathers of our land to awake to their sense of responsibility. In the name of Jesus our Saviour we pray. Amen.

## Too Busy to Sin

*"Having your conversation honest among the Gentiles: that, whereas they speak against you as evildoers, they may by your good works, which they shall behold, glorify God in the day of visitation."* — I Peter 2:12

Carrol called her friend on the phone and said some ugly things to her because she had the mistaken idea her friend had talked about her. So their friendship came to an end.

If you were busy being kind
Before you knew it you would find
You'd soon forget to think 'twas true
That someone was unkind to you.

If you were busy being glad
And cheering people who are sad,
Although your heart might ache a bit,
You'd soon forget to notice it.

If you were busy being good
And doing just the best you could
You'd not have time to blame some man
Who's doing just the best he can.

If you were busy being true
To what you know you ought to do,
You'd be so busy you'd forget
The blunders of the folks you've met.

If you were busy being right
You'd find yourslf too busy quite
To criticise your neighbor long
Because he's busy doing wrong.

*Prayer*: Our Father, as we come before thee, help us to put aside the tendency to criticize others. Let the sunshine of thy love and kindness be reflected in our dealings with others. For the sake of Jesus Christ we pray. Amen.

## The Peace Within

*"That he would grant you, according to the riches of his glory, to be strengthened with might by his Spirit in the inner man; That Christ may dwell in your hearts by faith.*
— Ephesians 3:16, 17

A wise man said, "Personality has the power to open many doors — but only character can keep them open."

I once knew a man who had a great talent for speaking in public. But — within he was like a raging torrent. If the speaker before him ran as much as a minute over his allotted time, he began to fume. If someone failed to bow and scrape to him as he walked to the platform he would become very angry. In no way did he show the inner peace that God expects Christians to have.

A man's a man who, knowing life is meant
For work, for work's own sake works on, content.
His head and hands, his heart's behest obey,
True as the sun and faithful as the day.
His task engages all he is or can,
And in its joy he feels himself — a man!
What'er his work, it is his only pride
To scant no measure and no weakness hide.

He hails as "Master"! Him and Him alone.
By whose achievements better grow his own.
A man's a man, and may, by self-control
And by his worth to Man, become — a useful soul.

*Prayer*: Father of all mankind, make us realize we need the inner peace given only by thee. Help us to serve others and in so doing to serve thee. In the name of one who gave his life for us, Jesus Christ, we pray. Amen.

## Let Us Number Our Days

*"So teach us to number our days, that we may apply our hearts unto wisdom."* — Psalm 90:12

One time we were all packed and ready to leave for our vacation.

"Just a few more moments while I run out to the hospital and make a last visit to one of our members," said my husband.

A boy driving too fast ran into our car at an intersection. The car was almost a total wreck but my husband was not seriously hurt.

This experience made us stop and think. This might have been my husband's last hour on earth. Any hour, any minute, may be our last hour or minute.

So — let us number our days, and apply our hearts to wisdom.
'Tis not for man to trifle! Life is brief,
    And sin is here.
Our age is but the falling of a leaf,
    A dropping tear.
We have no time to sport away the hours,
All must be earnest in a world like ours.

Not many lives, but only one have we —
    One, only one;
How sacred should that one life ever be —
    That narrow span!
Day after day filled up with blessed toil,
Hour after hour still bringing in new spoil.

                  — Horatius Bonar

*Prayer*: Dear Father, bless us when we have periods of waiting Illumine the spirits of thy people with thy love. Help us always to know thy will is best. In the name of Christ. Amen.

## God's Businessman

*"And he said unto them, How is it that ye sought me? wist ye not that I must be about my Father's business?"* — Luke 2:49

*"Not slothful in business; fervent in spirit; serving the Lord."* — Romans 12:11

Men dream about the time when their sons will enter the business world. God's son also had a business to enter. It was the business of establishing the kingdom of heaven on earth.

If you would be happy in the business world there are a few basic rules to follow. Jesus followed all of them.

Forget yourself and put your best into the job.
Keep an open-mind and be tolerant of others.
Serve others sincerely.
Learn to be practical.
Love your work and think of it as important.
Be true to lofty ideals.
Learn something daily.
Be enthusiastic.

Never forget that you are a child of the King and give your allegiance to Him first.

*Prayer:* Our Father, who guides our steps each day, as we go about our daily work help us to say as David of old: "I will lift up mine eyes unto the hills, from whence cometh my help." In the name of the giver of all help. Amen.

## Checking our Baggage

*"And Moses took the bones of Joseph with him; for he had straitly sworn the children of Israel, saying, God will surely visit you; and ye shall carry up my bones away hence with you."* — Exodus 13:19

It is sometimes hard to get people traveling on the train or bus to check their baggage. Some want it where they can "get at it" during the entire trip. A boy I knew taking his first bus trip failed to check his bag. He carefully placed it on the shelf over his head. At one of the bus stops he got off to look around. When he arrived home he reached for his bag — and it was not on the shelf. The bag was never found. The boy determined that if he ever took another trip he would check his baggage.

We all take out into the world with us each day things we might better check. For example, we would do well to check and forget many frets and worries. Why don't we "take them to the Lord and leave them there"?

If we ask God to work out our problems and then go on about our work we may rest assured he will work them out for us.

There are, however, some things we should take along and never check: a happy smile, a cheerful word of greeting, a helping hand for those about us. These are so easily carried along. Let's keep them with us.

> Build a little fence of trust
>    Around today;
> Fill the space with loving deeds,
>    And therein stay.
> Look not through the sheltering bars
>    Upon tomorrow;
> God will help thee bear what comes
>    Of joy or sorrow.

> — Mary Frances Butts

*Prayer*: Our Heavenly Father, we desire an abundance of thy grace. Use us to advance thy kingdom. We pray in the name of our Lord. Amen.